Sunset Boulevard

Sunset Boulevard

Cruising the Heart of Los Angeles

Amy Dawes

Los Angeles Times
BOOKS

TO MY PARENTS, BOB AND ANNETTE,
FOR MOVING US TO LOS ANGELES,
AND TO BILLY, FOR MAKING IT HOME.

Los Angeles Times
BOOKS

Editor: Carla Lazzareschi
Designer: Michael Diehl
Photo Researcher: Stacey Rain Strickler
Copy Editor: Steven R. Hawkins
Image Restoration: Molly Bosted
Map Rendering: Brian Zick

ISBN: 1-883792-62-2
Copyright: Los Angeles Times 2002
Published by the Los Angeles Times
202 West First Street, Los Angeles, CA 90012

First printing May 2002
Printed in China

Los Angeles Times

Publisher: John P. Puerner
Editor: John S. Carroll
Book Development General Manager: Carla Lazzareschi

· ·
A theatrical production of "Sunset Boulevard" played
at the Pantages Theatre (on Hollywood Boulevard)
in 1999.

Contents

Introduction

There isn't a street in the world like Sunset Boulevard. Dazzling and decadent, disturbing and dangerous, bleak at one end and beautiful at the other, it stretches all the way from downtown Los Angeles to the Pacific Ocean. In all, its nearly 23 miles encompass the full spectrum—from magical legend to gritty reality—that makes the City of Angels what it is.

Studded with historic buildings and famous homes, well-known nightspots and diverse neighborhoods both coveted and struggling, Sunset Boulevard has inspired a classic movie, a hit Broadway musical, and countless pilgrimages by visitors from all over the world. Some seek it out because its name is legendary, with little idea of what to expect. Others zero in on the pop culture of the Sunset Strip or the mansions of Beverly Hills. Still others have heard that one of the truest ways to experience Los Angeles is to drive Sunset Boulevard from end to end, starting at the old Plaza, the city's historic birthplace near Union Station, and proceeding all the way to the blue frontier of the Pacific.

Indeed, from the edge of Chinatown to the heart of bohemian Silver Lake to the leafy exclusivity of Bel-Air and the sea breezes of bluff-top Pacific Palisades, it's possible in a single day to absorb—from this fabled thoroughfare alone—an amazing overview of Los Angeles past and present. Such a journey deserves more than the visual blur seen from a speeding car. It deserves a rich understanding, not just of what's there but of what isn't any longer—and why.

And all the better if the years can be peeled back to reveal Los Angeles as it was at the turn of the century, when Sunset Boulevard was carved through the hills of Echo Park and horse-and-carriage traffic clipped gaily alongside the Red Car trolleys. Or later, in the 1920s and 1930s, when rapidly proliferating automobiles tootled along Sunset, carrying ridiculously lucky real estate developers and giddy Hollywood hopefuls. Or later still, in the mid-1960s, when runaways and flower children crowded the sidewalks and rebellious kids clashed with repressive cops in a riot on the Sunset Strip.

This book intends to be a guide to the sights, sounds, experiences, and lost legends of Sunset Boulevard, to landmarks both famous and scarcely recognized, to stories oft-told and hidden histories all but forgotten.

It proceeds geographically, from east to west, exploring neighborhoods and linking the present and the past. It invites along people who have shaped the boulevard and lent it their dreams and energy, people like Aimee Semple McPherson and Mack Sennett, Walt Disney and D.W. Griffith, Billy Wilder and Marilyn Monroe, Billy Wilkerson and Mickey Cohen, Will Rogers and Ronald Reagan. It describes the misdeeds too, the

....

Opposite: A Red Car trolley passes through Echo Park on Sunset Boulevard where it cuts through steep hills near Coronado Street, circa 1915. The house at the top of the photo still stands there today, though the Red Car system was long ago dismantled.

people whose twisted scandals and sorry ends haunt this storied street. It rolls down the window on sounds like Vin Scully announcing the Dodgers in a pennant year, garage bands working out new rock music in Silver Lake, and 1930s composer Harold Arlen feverishly humming and scribbling the melody to "Somewhere Over the Rainbow" at a fabled malt shop on the Sunset Strip.

You'll hear the world's most famous street noise the way the boulevard hears it, the way Raymond Chandler heard it, from the drunken laughter of a wild starlet, to the screams of police sirens racing to a suicide scene, to the whisper of dry eucalyptus leaves waiting to ignite in a super-heated Santa Ana. You'll see the whole thing—the details and the big, blazing picture—the way the Hollywood sign sees it, standing up on that hill stoic and benign, wait-

ing to preside over another fresh outrage or another paradisiacal day.

It's Sunset Boulevard, after all—it's not just any street in any town. Whether this is your city, or merely one you're visiting, may this book help launch your own rich and personal discovery of the boulevard, and may you never tire of spending time along this fabled street of dreams.

Birth of a Boulevard

Sunset Boulevard was born right alongside the city of Los Angeles, in a dusty settlement near the river where a few mud huts and a rude plaza were dubbed El Pueblo de Los Angeles in 1781. Then, the road that would become world famous was just a wide dirt path leading to a cow pasture to the west. And it remained so for nearly 100 years.

But by the late 1880s, this broad, dusty ribbon was being extended further west to link up with wagon trails coming in from nearby farms. As homesteaders forged into the hills that would become Echo Park, the crude thoroughfare leading back to the Plaza grew in importance. Sunset Boulevard was first recorded in city street department documents in 1888, and thereafter its growth was chronicled incrementally as it was graded, paved and pushed further west.

Its hauntingly evocative name is generally credited to a flash of inspiration by an unknown city employee, who probably noted how the setting sun shines into the eyes of a traveler going westward late in the day. Regardless, no one could have known then how famous the name would become, or all that Sunset Boulevard would come to encompass and represent.

Nor could anyone have known the phenomenal span it would one day cover. As the city grew, filling in the vast spaces between downtown and the sea, so did the

....

This wooden cross, still in place on Olvera Street, marks the site of the founding of the city. Opposite: The rural corner of what would become Laurel Canyon and Sunset boulevards in West Hollywood, looking east, circa 1905.

boulevard, picking up speed in the first and second decades of the new century.

Out at the coast, the bucolic community of Pacific Palisades was beginning to attract settlers. However, it wasn't until January 1926 that Sunset Boulevard was pushed through the canyons to link up with an existing road leading to the ocean, and the great artery was at last complete. The Pacific Palisades portion of the thoroughfare had previously been called Beverly Bou-

levard, but the name Sunset Boulevard had acquired a romance that developers sought to capitalize on. In 1934 they succeeded in removing the name Beverly so that the entire stretch could be called Sunset.

Sunset Boulevard ran from downtown near the city's birthplace to the ocean for nearly 60 years. Then, in 1993, several blocks at the eastern end were renamed to honor Cesar Chavez, the late activist for the rights of Mexican-American farm

How Long Is It?

At 22.4 miles, Sunset Boulevard is the second-longest street in Los Angeles. (It was formerly nearly 24 miles long, before a stretch at its eastern end was renamed to honor Cesar Chavez, late founder of the United Farm Workers of America.)

Only Sepulveda Boulevard is longer, measuring in at 25.4 miles within the city limits of Los Angeles. (In its entirety, from Sepulveda Dam in the San Fernando Valley to the harbor at San Pedro, Sepulveda Boulevard runs a whopping 57 miles.)

Hollywood Boulevard, nearly as famous as Sunset, covers only 4.7 miles.

Wilshire Boulevard, which parallels Sunset from downtown to the ocean, takes a much straighter route and gets there in 15.8 miles.

workers, and merged on city maps with the former Brooklyn Avenue running through East Los Angeles. Thus the present-day Sunset Boulevard begins officially at Figueroa Street, several blocks west of the Plaza. ⑤

620—EL PASO DE LOS ANGELES "THE PATHWAY OF THE ANGELS"

OLVERA STREET, LOS ANGELES, CALIFORNIA

Union Station, El Pueblo, and Chinatown

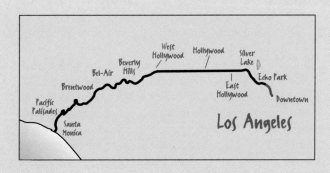

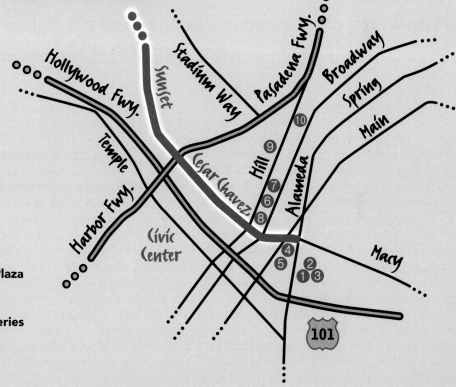

1. **Union Station**

2. **Old Chinatown**

3. **MTA Transit Plaza**

4. **Philippe's Restaurant**

5. **El Pueblo Historical Monument, Olvera Street, Chinese American Museum**

6. **New Chinatown**

7. **East Gate to Central Plaza**

8. **Gateway Dragons**

9. **Chung King Road galleries**

10. **Chinese Heritage and Visitors Center**

The elegant downtown railway station,

opened in 1939 very close to the original starting point of Sunset Boulevard, is the City of Angels' gateway to the past—a link to the bustling war years and the stylish, storied era captured in film noir and Raymond Chandler novels.

But it's also a monument to the city's transportation future, housing the MTA's opulent new office tower and a veritable theme park of beguiling public art. Now serving Amtrak rail travelers and the city's Metrolink and subway lines, Union Station has survived decades of decline and neglect to emerge with a new role.

Today, the handsomely restored depot offers a chance to experience Los Angeles much the way it looked during the 1940s, when this gem of fused architectural styles inspired the first impression of the growing city for a generation of arrivals.

City fathers wanted the station's design to serve the tourism industry by emphasizing what they believed were the area's most marketable elements—its climate and sunshine, Spanish heritage, and exotic West Coast mystique.

Arriving passengers move quickly out-of-doors from the central terminal—where California sunshine filters in through tall, arched windows fitted with amber cathedral glass—onto sun-splashed patios planted with olive and pepper trees. To people coming in from Chicago or New York in the dead of winter, it could not have been clearer that they had reached the fabled El Dorado of the West.

Then, as now, the dramatic main waiting room featured gleaming floors of Spanish red tile; deep, boxy leather settees; and a richly patterned, cathedral-style ceiling offset by great rounded arches. Station noise was hushed by innovative acoustic tiles in the upper walls and ceilings that allow passengers to actually understand departure announcements.

The former Fred Harvey restaurant—part of a chain where rail passengers could count on quick service from uniformed "Harvey Girls"—closed in the 1960s. But outside the station and across Alameda Street is Philippe the Original, a casual, sawdust-on-the-floor eatery in operation since 1908. There, you can still get a French dip sandwich and a 9-cent cup of coffee, just as in the 1940s.

Frequently used for filming, the terminal was the site of the 1950 suspense thriller *Union Station*, starring William Holden, as well as scenes in *Bugsy*, *Rain Man*, *The Way We Were*, and *Blade Runner*, among others.

At the rear of the station is the vaunted new $300-million office tower and Transit Plaza of the MTA, billed as the city's "transportation hub for the 21st century." It contains a don't-miss collection of public art commissioned when the facilities opened in 1995.

The office tower, tricked out in Italian granite and swank furniture, stirred controversy upon its debut. Some perceived it as a slap in the face to commuters who rely on

....

Opposite: The waiting room at Union Station shortly after its 1939 opening.

bus service that they complain is under-funded and overcrowded. Nick Patsouras, the transit official for whom the Plaza is named, countered the outcry by insisting that the MTA "owed it to the citizens of Los Angeles" to create the luxurious public space, so by all means, take advantage.

The artworks integrated throughout the complex were funded by a city ordinance mandating that one percent of the budget for public buildings be set aside for public art. In this case, that came to $3 million and involved 17 artists and architects, plus dozens of technicians and construction specialists.

The MTA tower features four striking landscape murals by artist James Doolin. Depicting Los Angeles in 1870, 1910, 1960, and 2000, they offer dramatic snapshots of how the changing transportation picture has defined the city.

In the Plaza's East Portal, a multipart piece titled "City of Dreams, River of History" features a floor inlaid with bronze images of trout, turtles, and flora. A 79-by-22-foot mural by Richard Wyatt depicts the multiethnic faces of L.A.'s original settlers and modern citizens.

May Sun's "River Bench," at the rear of the station, pays homage to Los Angeles'

original Chinatown, a web of narrow streets and alleys that was razed to make way for Union Station. Construction workers in the 1930s and again in the 1980s, when a subway line was brought to the train station, uncovered hundreds of artifacts from Old Chinatown's heyday. They range from porcelain tea cups and rice bowls to Chinese coins, gambling dominoes, opium pipe bowls, and dentures.

Among the many other artworks is a fanciful and fascinating piece by artist Bill Bell, a former MIT professor. The installation features vertical light sticks that create a changing stream of optical illusions, from the image of a passing freight train—complete with whistle blast—to celebrity faces peering out from fast-moving passenger cars.

Union Station is usually described as "the last of the great train stations." Justifiably so. By the time the station opened in 1939, the "golden age" of railroading had nearly ended. But the fact Union Station even opened is amazing. The railroads, which for decades had been powerful corporate giants with a key role in attracting settlers to Los Angeles and expanding its

----

Opposite: A mural by James Doolin commemorates the arrival of the first railroad train in Los Angeles in 1870.

commercial reach, resisted being forced to build the new station and fought the city in the courts for more than 15 years.

The saga starts in the first decade of the 20th century with three railroads—the Southern Pacific, Santa Fe, and Union Pacific—offering service in and out of downtown Los Angeles—each with its own terminal. By 1915, city leaders were fed up with the traffic tie-ups caused by the crisscrossing tracks of the independent concerns, and self-conscious about the poor first impression made on arrivals at the various grimy train depots. (For decades before Union Station was built, movie stars and other VIPS would arrive and depart Los Angeles from the Pasadena station, which was considered far more gracious and photogenic.)

Extravagant train stations—such as the original Pennsylvania Station in New York—were considered status symbols by emerging cities of the day. But the railroads, rather than taxpayers, had paid to construct them. In 1915, the city of Los Angeles filed a complaint with the railroad commission to force the railroads to construct a "union station" that would consolidate their operations in one grand terminal. The railroads fought the action.

Suits and countersuits were filed. The dispute dragged on for more than 15 years before it landed in the U.S. Supreme Court, which decided in favor of the city in 1931. After Mayor Frank Shaw kicked in $1 million in public funds, the railroads decided to play ball.

A committee of architects selected by all three railroads set to work. The design team was led by consulting architects John Parkinson and Donald Parkinson, who had helped create City Hall and the Art Deco-style Bullocks Wilshire department store. With so many cooks in the kitchen, many observers were skeptical, but the station that emerged won them over.

With an architectural style officially described as Spanish Colonial Revival with Art Deco elements, the station suggests a Spanish mission brought gently into the modern age. Its distinctive 135-foot clock tower, topped with a Moorish finial, became an instant Los Angeles landmark.

Opening ceremonies in May 1939 lasted three days. An extravaganza, called Romance of the Rails, was staged right on the tracks. A parade came down Alameda Street, with floats, marching bands, and Army tanks. At 5:30 a.m. on Friday, May 7, Southern Pacific's Imperial

rolled into the station—the first train carrying paying passengers to arrive at Los Angeles Union Station.

The country's entry into World War II in 1941 transformed Union Station, quickly turning it into the transportation hub for the region's military and defense industry. Soldiers, Marines, sailors, factory workers, and supplies flowed in and out of the station, as Southern California supplied a third of all U.S. aircraft produced during the war. At the peak of the war years, the station handled 100 trains a day, up from 66 a day when it opened, taxing the terminal to its limit.

With their weekend passes, military personnel from units throughout California arrived knowing just where they wanted to go—out the doors to ride the Red Cars or their thumbs down Sunset Boulevard to Hollywood, where a club called the Hollywood Canteen, at the corner of Sunset and Cahuenga Boulevard, offered legendary good times. Started by movie stars Bette Davis and Jane Russell, along with merchants and civic leaders with the idea of doing their bit for the war effort, the club more than made up for its no-alcohol policy by refusing to admit military brass; only enlisted men and women could enter. Many Hollywood stars, including Dorothy Lam-

our, Danny Thomas, Helen Hayes, Mickey Rooney, Dinah Shore, and Red Skelton, appeared in volunteer shifts to entertain, serve refreshments, and wash dishes.

Despite a 20-year heyday, Union Station had been born too late for its pivotal position to last. Highways were being improved, Los Angeles International Airport was coming of age, and jetliners were overtaking trains as the preferred method of travel. By 1958, only 46 daily trains came into Union Station. By 1967, the number was down to 30. Unlike in many East Coast stations, there was no rail commuter traffic to keep the station alive.

In 1971, Amtrak began operating national passenger service from Union Station. That same year, Union Station was declared a historic cultural monument—just 32 years after it opened. In 1990, Metrolink began commuter rail operations, bringing people from points all over the region into downtown through Union Station. And since 1993, the Metro Red Line subway, which now extends into

the heart of Hollywood and out to the San Fernando Valley, has brought even more passengers to its eastern terminus at Union Station.

Although these services don't yet bring in the crowds that once passed through the terminal, commuter traffic is building and Union Station is once again enjoying an active role in the region's transportation.

....

Union Station, as seen from Alameda Street, during opening day celebrations May 7, 1939. The station's first passenger train had arrived at 5:30 a.m. earlier that day. Opposite: The dirt path that became Sunset Boulevard originated at El Pueblo, shown here in 1860.

Across Alameda Street from

Union Station stands the El Pueblo Historical Monument, the birthplace of the city, an area encompassing the old Plaza, Olvera Street, and 27 historic structures. Among them are Pico House, constructed in 1869 as the first three-story building in Los Angeles; the Avila Adobe, the city's oldest adobe structure; and the red brick Sepulveda House, a former boarding residence built in 1887.

Located at 662 North Main Street, the Sepulveda House includes a visitor center that offers free walking-tour maps. It also offers free docent-guided tours several times daily, Tuesday through Saturday.

The historic area—which got a cleanup and partial restoration in time for the Democratic National Convention in 2000—offers a glimpse into an earlier way of life in Los Angeles. The central bandstand, shaded by Moreton Bay fig trees planted in the 1870s, often features mariachis or folkloric dancers on weekends and holidays. The Plaza Catholic church, the oldest church in the city, is lively with weddings and baptisms nearly every weekend. Nightly candlelit processions called Las Posadas take place the week before Christmas. The Saturday before Easter brings the Blessing of the Animals, in which residents line up to have a priest anoint their pets with prayer.

Brick-paved Olvera Street, created in the 1930s to draw tourists, is a pedestrian area thick with marketplace stalls and food booths in the traditional Mexican style. Mariachi bands frequently serenade visitors enjoying cocktails on restaurant patios.

Among other highlights in the monument area is the 18-by-80-foot mural "America Tropical," painted in 1932 by

David Alfaro Siqueiros on an exterior wall of the Italian Hall overlooking Olvera Street. The mural was quickly whitewashed over because its themes, depicting the exploitation of Mexican labor and hinting at a violent revolt

603 THE PLAZA CHURCH, LOS ANGELES, CALIFORNIA

John Hughes Photo

against the United States, were seen as politically incendiary. Arts preservationists have waged a long campaign to uncover the image, and it is now partly visible.

Nearby is the newly reopened Garnier building, dating from 1890, that will house the new Chinese American Museum slated to open in 2003.

. . . .

Above: The Plaza in the 1930s. Left: The Plaza Church, the oldest Roman Catholic church in Los Angeles. Opposite: Celebrations of Mexican culture and crafts abound on Olvera Street within the El Pueblo Historical Monument.

Chinatown

Old Chinatown in Los Angeles

sprang up in the mid-1800s and was home to about 200 men, many of whom had traveled to the United States to help build the railroads. Originally located primarily along Calle de Los Negroes, a shabby back street

just east of the area where the city's first band of 44 settlers encamped, the community evolved into a web of narrow streets and alleys that became the not-so-secret home to much of Los Angeles' vice in the early 20th century.

From its earliest days, Chinatown's residents organized in tightly knit clubs known as "tongs" to protect themselves and their business interests. Competitive as well as protective, the clubs frequently sparred, often with deadly consequences. In 1870, a particularly heated clash between two of these tongs resulted in the death of a white police officer who was trying to settle it. The death ignited simmering racial animosity toward the Chinese, and a white mob gathered in Chinatown. Within five hours, 19 Chinese men and boys had been murdered, 15 of them hung. (Nearly a dozen whites, including the sheriff, had tried to calm the mob, to no avail.) The event, known as the Chinese Massacre, was decried in newspapers across the country and brought unflattering attention to the muddy village of Los Angeles.

No wonder the residents of Chinatown weren't keen on outsiders. Feared and mistrusted by many whites, who focused more on the jobs the Chinese might "steal" than the labor they contributed, many developed their own underground economies as a means of survival.

By the turn of the century, Old Chinatown was home to as many as 100 opium smoking dens, operating mostly in back rooms reached through maze-like streets. After opium was outlawed in 1912, the price increased. So did the trade. As many as 10,000 half-pound tins a year were soon being delivered to the heart of the action— at the downtown corner of Los Angeles and

....

Left: Tourists in 1939 at China City, a short-lived attraction near New Chinatown. Top: The opium trade flourished in Old Chinatown, and drug smoking, through elongated pipes, was open. Opposite: Low Chen, owner of the Bamboo Inn in China City in the 1940s.

Commercial streets—until the 1930s, when the Feds cracked down.

Los Angeles police officers had been looking the other way—for a price, of course. Police corruption was rampant throughout the city, but nowhere more so than in Chinatown, where as much as $400,000 a year was supposedly passing into official hands to protect illegal doings. And it wasn't just drugs. Gambling and prostitution were as rampant. The clatter of mahjongg tiles could be heard throughout the old quarter, and wagers were taken on exotic games like tse-far, which involved naming a hidden tile by answering a riddle. Prostitution took root due to a scarcity of women in the early settlement, but thrived over the decades in the shambling hotels near the railroad tracks.

In the 1920s, the tongs waged open warfare to protect their interests—a West Coast, Chinese-style version of the organized crime violence that was to come in Chicago and New York. Newspaper accounts tell of gangs like the Hop Sing and the Bing Kong shooting it out amid a Chinese New Year celebration, of tong leaders being assassinated while playing dominoes or fan-tan. By the late 1920s, however, the LAPD's Chinatown Detail, under Police Chief Jim Davis, strong-armed the tongs into submission—or at least discretion. A few years later, city officials solved their crime problem once and for all. They simply erected Union Station atop Old Chinatown.

Vice was only one aspect of the Chinatown story. The Chinese you didn't read about in the newspapers were busy launching grocery stores, restaurants, and other businesses. Many worked as laundrymen, vegetable growers, and road builders. Thousands labored to build the difficult San Fernando railway tunnel, which brought the first outside railroad link to Los Angeles, changing the city's fortunes. Chinese workers also helped plant, tend, harvest, and can produce, which was shipped out on rail routes they helped construct. All told, in the 19th century and even into the early 20th century, the toughest construction jobs in the state—the building of dams, the digging of irrigation channels, the clearing of swamps—were completed primarily with Chinese labor.

In Old Chinatown's heyday, from 1890

to 1910, it had a Chinese opera theater, three temples, and its own newspaper. As the number of female residents increased and families with children were established, so too were the bonds and institutions that began to shape the Chinese community.

Food was the main draw for outsiders. The smells of chow mein and chop suey—the latter invented on these shores—enticed many downtown residents and workers into the Chinese quarter, often to restaurants situated on the second floor, where rents were cheaper. A white storekeeper living in Chinatown named Tom Gubbins, or "Ah Tom," spoke 35 Chinese dialects and served as an unofficial liaison between the two communities. When Hollywood called for "Orientals" as extras in war movies, Gubbins helped agent many of his neighbors into $5-a-day jobs.

But Old Chinatown was destined to tumble. The area had been marked by the city for its ambitious new railroad station, and when the project commenced in the mid-1930s, residents were displaced. Their homes, businesses, and meeting halls were razed, wiping out a nearly century-old community. Only the Garnier building, dating from 1890, remains—and even that was cut in half to accommodate freeway construction in the 1950s. It was slated to become home to the new Chinese American Museum in 2003.

New Chinatown

Easy to visit from Sunset Boulevard, which borders its southern edge, today's Chinatown is a charming but slightly faded historic quarter with broad streets and fantasy architecture that serves as one of L.A.'s more tantalizing links to a vanishing past. But like so much of older Los Angeles, it too is undergoing significant transformation.

New Chinatown, as it's been called

since opening in 1938, was created as Union Station was rising over the bones of the city's original Chinese settlement just a few blocks away. This easily walkable neighborhood covers a quarter square mile and is home to about 15,000 residents. About two-thirds are Chinese; the rest are from Cambodia, Malaysia, Vietnam, and elsewhere.

Chinatown welcomes visitors, most of whom come to enjoy its parades, restaurants, and *dim sum* feasts, or to explore herbalist shops or import stores filled with exotic goods and trinkets. In recent years, an art scene has sprung up in galleries along Chung King Road, bringing a new energy and some splashy opening night parties into the mix.

On Broadway just north of Cesar E. Chavez Avenue, a renamed section of Sunset Boulevard, an elaborate archway depicting two 40-foot gold dragons greets visitors. Called the "Gateway to Chinatown," the metal sculpture monument was designed by Chinese-born architect Rupert Mok and erected in July 2001. Rising 43 feet

••••••••••••••••••••••

A statue of Sun Yat-Sen stands in the Central Plaza of New Chinatown. Opposite, left: The Golden Pagoda restaurant on Broadway. Opposite, right: Chung King Road in New Chinatown.

above the ground, the dragons meet in the "sky" over Broadway; an opaque fiberglass pearl representing longevity and prosperity appears to float between them.

Chinatown's picturesque Central Plaza runs along Broadway between College and Bernard streets, and can be entered through the elaborate arch of its East Gate. Ringed with import shops and buildings decorated with whimsical Chinese flourishes designed to appeal to tourists, the plaza is quiet compared to its heyday. Nevertheless, it still offers a beguiling and transporting glimpse into a faraway culture.

There's a wishing well where a well-aimed coin might bring romance, health, or a better run of luck. In the 1940s, the well was called the Seven Star Sacred Caverns, and actress Anna May Wong planted a willow tree here to draw publicity. A neon Buddha sign decorates the R.G. Louie company, and nearby is a dragon mural done in 1984 by Fu-Ding Cheng. The statue in the Plaza is a likeness of Sun Yat-Sen, founder of the Chinese Republic, who was honored at a banquet in Old Chinatown in 1905 during a secret visit to Los Angeles.

Chinatown's public art is best discovered by following a walking tour map available from the nearby Chinese Historical

Society (415 Bernard Street), which houses a free museum displaying artifacts and photographs of early Chinese American life in Los Angeles.

New Chinatown was cause for great pride in the Chinese community when it opened on June 25, 1938. The streets were jammed; bands played and youths paraded in native costume. People danced to American music by the light of paper lanterns until well past midnight, and so many fireworks were set off that the streets the next day were carpeted in red paper.

What was being celebrated? Self-sufficiency. The land and buildings of the new district were entirely owned by Chinese merchants and family associations, purchased with money they had raised among themselves.

In the crisis surrounding the forced relocation of the Chinese community from its home in the Union Station area, a local hero had emerged— Peter SooHoo, a University of Southern California engineering graduate born and raised in Old Chinatown. A gifted coalition builder, SooHoo had helped secure the new site and built support for a shared vision of the first planned Chinatown.

Because Old Chinatown had been perceived by many as an insular, crime-ridden neighborhood that only the more adventurous tourists dared to penetrate, the merchants of New Chinatown wanted to dispel that image and attract commerce from all cultures. To that end, they called for fire-safe modern buildings and wide, open streets, and hired architects Eric Webster and Adrian Wilson to create buildings that would embrace the cultures of both their native and adopted countries.

This unique architecture, still largely in place today, blends Chinese ornamental flourishes with modern American elements for a Disney-esque effect. Derided as kitschy by some, the style is treasured by others as a nostalgic link to a bygone era. Regardless, the merchants' plan was a hit. By its second anniversary, the plaza was attracting 20,000 visitors per week, and its popularity continued to grow.

In the 1950s, Chinatown was a major tourist attraction. Visitors thronged over from Union Station, some riding rickshaws sent by merchants. Elaborate, enchanting

....

A menu cover from the Forbidden Palace in New Chinatown. Opposite: Youngsters enjoy a Chinese New Year's parade.

restaurants, such as Golden Pagoda and Hop Louie, catered to outsiders and their newfound thirst for the Orient, which had been stimulated by movies like *The Good Earth* (1937). Nightclubs thrived, livened up by visitors from Hollywood, including Frank Sinatra, Dean Martin, and their cronies. Businesses stayed open until one or two in the morning.

But by the mid-1960s, Chinatown's popularity as a tourist attraction and nightlife scene was waning. The new youth culture saw the community as largely irrelevant and clichéd, and the war in Vietnam made Asia seem anything but romantic. Furthermore, new immigrants were arriving who wanted their full share of the American Dream. Chinatown, as it had been known for decades, would be irrevocably changed.

In the 1970s, changing immigration laws brought a wave of middle-class and professional Asian immigrants to Los Angeles, in place of the struggling laborers who had previously flocked to these shores. This new group disdained the city core, dreaming instead of suburban houses and two-car garages.

A Chinese-American real estate agent named Frederic Hsieh began aggressively luring them to the San Gabriel Valley. Today, Monterey Park and surrounding towns have the largest Chinese population in Southern California. Affluence and education are the hallmarks of this suburban enclave. Hundreds of millionaires from China, Taiwan, and Hong Kong were lured over by a 1991 federal program that promised legal immigrant status to a foreigner who would invest $1 million in a business that could create at least 10 full-time jobs.

The Chinatown that was left behind suffered a loss of vitality, population, and commerce. As refugees from the war in Vietnam and Cambodia arrived, settling in L.A.'s downtown core, Chinatown's merchants found they could best survive by catering to them rather than to American tourists.

Today Chinatown is marked by a cultural diversity that has given the community a more vibrant, energetic, and creative

Check it out: Union Station, El Pueblo, and Chinatown

Union Station

Food and Drink

Traxx, in Union Station at Los Angeles and Alameda streets, (213) 625-1999. Swank bar and restaurant featuring nouveau California cuisine.

Philippe the Original, corner of Alameda and Ord streets (across from Union Station), (213) 628-3781. Casual, atmospheric eatery, offering French dip sandwiches and 9-cent cups of coffee since 1908.

Tours

Los Angeles Conservancy, (213) 623-CITY (call on weekdays). Guided walking tours of Union Station, third and fourth Saturday morning each month. $8.

Angel City Tours, (310) 470-4463. Walking tours every Saturday, including Union Station, MTA Plaza, and other downtown locales. $12.50.

El Adobe Plaza and Olvera Street

Food and Drink

La Golondrina, West-17 Olvera Street, (213) 628-4349. Cadillac margaritas, Mexican food, strolling mariachis, prime people-watching.

Tours

Visitor Center at Sepulveda House, 662 North Main Street, (213) 628-1274. Free tours several times daily, Tuesdays–Saturdays.

Cinco de Mayo, Mexican Independence Day celebration, (213) 628-1274. Live music, dancing, food.

Chinatown

Food and Drink

ABC Seafood, 205 Ord Street, (213) 680-2887. Busy, authentic Hong Kong-style seafood house, popular dim sum spot.

Empress Pavilion, 988 North Hill Street, (213) 617-9898. Capacious room, Chinese specialties, hugely popular for dim sum brunch on weekends.

Hop Louie, 950 Mei Ling Way, (213) 628-4244. Atmospheric 1941 landmark, formerly the Golden Pagoda. Restaurant and bar, exotic drinks.

Yang Chow, 819 North Broadway, (213) 625-0811. Mandarin and Szechuan specialties since the 1970s.

Pho 79, 727 North Broadway, (213) 625-7026. Casual, popular Vietnamese eatery.

Phoenix Bakery, 969 North Broadway, (213) 628-4642. Chinese and American pastries since 1938. Renowned for strawberry whipped-cream birthday cakes—a childhood tradition for many.

Specialty Shopping

Wing Hop Fung Ginseng and **China Products Center**, 727 North Broadway, (213) 626-7200. Huge selection of herbs, roots, teas, and remedies. Pharmacist and acupuncturist on the premises.

Night Life

Grand Star, 933 North Broadway, (213) 626-2285. Since 1946, kitschy hang for fun-loving regulars, tourists. Karaoke weeknights until 2 a.m., sing-along jazz band on weekends. Exotic drinks, restaurant.

Museums and Special Events

Chinese Heritage and Visitors Center, 411-415 Bernard Street, (323) 222-1918. Open Sundays only, noon-4 p.m. Photos, artifacts, info on Chinese-American experience in the region. Free.

Chinese American Museum, to open in 2003 in historic 1890 Garnier building, 423 North Los Angeles Street, (213) 626-5240. Three-level museum will feature scale model of Old Chinatown, other exhibits and collections.

Chinese New Year and **Golden Dragon Parade**, annual events held late January, mid-February. Call Chinese Chamber of Commerce for exact date, (213) 617-0396. Dragon dancers, floats, firecrackers, carnival. Draws up to 50,000 spectators.

Firecracker 5K/10K Run, (323) 256-1363. Annual exertion through hilly Chinatown corresponds with Chinese New Year celebration.

The Chinatown Art Scene

Since January 1999, more than half a dozen galleries have opened on Chung King Road, and more spaces are being renovated. Art openings have partygoers and scene-makers back in Chinatown in a way not remembered since the 1980s, when punk rock bloomed at clubs like Madame Wong's and the Hong Kong Cafe.

The current gallery lineup includes China Art Objects, INMO, the Black Dragon Society, Goldman Tevis, Dianepreuss, Lord Mori, and the Electronic Orphanage, all on Chung King Road, and Acuna-Hansen, around the corner at 427 Bernard Street. Contemporary, avant-garde, and multimedia art are emphasized, with no particular allegiance to Asian culture. Galleries tend to be open Thursdays, Fridays, and weekends only.

character. Immigrants from Cambodia, Malaysia and Vietnam—many of them ethnic Chinese—own more than 50 percent of the businesses. Nearly 20 percent of residents are Latino. And for the first time since the 19th century, when a little Italy took root in the area, a handful of whites are moving in.

The venerable Capitol Milling Co. on Spring Street is being renovated into live-work space for artists and high-tech firms. And artists are drifting over from the downtown loft scene into buildings left empty from suburban flight. While some have mourned the loss of the community's singularly Chinese flavor, a certain pragmatism has taken hold. "There's been some apprehension about that, but people are recognizing that the times are changing, and it's better to let these buildings be active than to lie in the doldrums," said Eugene Moy, a docent at the Chinese Historical Society.

Community business leaders are actively promoting the neighborhood's revival. In mid-2000, they drew up a plan to reverse a decade of benign neglect by sprucing up the district and beginning anew to market it to tourists. And by 2003, the Metro blue line to Pasadena will stop in Chinatown, bringing it into the pathway of countless commuters and rail travelers. S

Echo Park

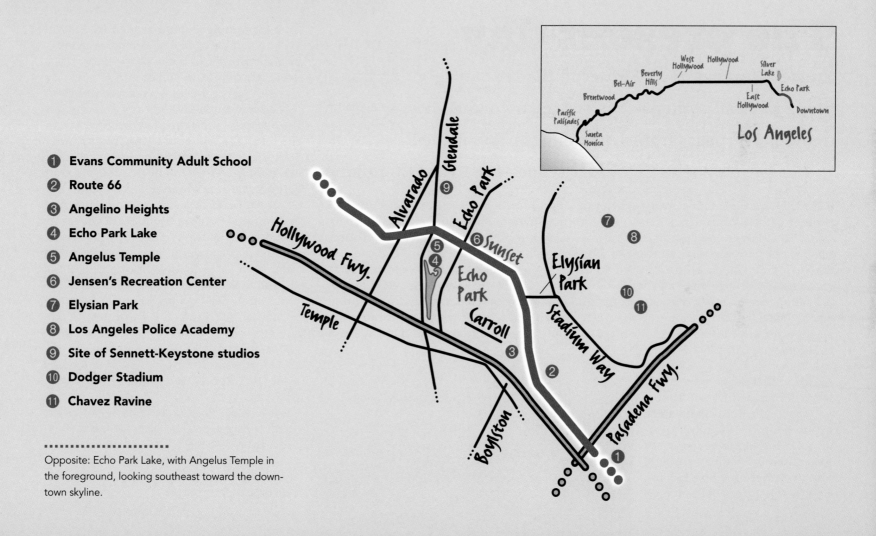

1. Evans Community Adult School
2. Route 66
3. Angelino Heights
4. Echo Park Lake
5. Angelus Temple
6. Jensen's Recreation Center
7. Elysian Park
8. Los Angeles Police Academy
9. Site of Sennett-Keystone studios
10. Dodger Stadium
11. Chavez Ravine

Opposite: Echo Park Lake, with Angelus Temple in the foreground, looking southeast toward the downtown skyline.

The present-day starting point of Sunset Boulevard at Figueroa Street can seem strikingly bleak at first glance—trash-strewn vacant lots, a roaring freeway overpass, graffiti, barrenness, and neglect.

But there's poetry in the landscape—the Evans Community

Adult School on the northwest corner of Sunset and Figueroa is a kind of West Coast Ellis Island, serving immigrants to Los Angeles. Free classes in English, citizenship and job skills are offered to as many as 15,000 students each semester in 225 jam-packed classes that run six days a week. There's scarcely an edifice in L.A. that better symbolizes the entry point to the American Dream.

This very stretch of Sunset rolling westward into Echo Park is part of historic Route 66, the legendary 2,448-mile artery built in 1926 from Chicago to L.A. and made famous in literature by John Steinbeck and Jack Kerouac and in song by Chuck Berry. (Route 66

merges with Sunset Boulevard after skipping in from Pasadena to the east; then, at the juncture with Santa Monica Boulevard, it follows that path to the ocean.)

A few blocks further west, the vibrancy and color of the Echo Park neighborhood—one of the city's oldest and most historic and, to this day, an authentic urban melting pot—begin to take hold. This section of

Sunset, completed and graded by around 1905, was one of the toughest and most costly stretches to build, particularly in the area approaching Coronado Street. As many as 100 teams of horses were required to perform the heavy work of gouging out the hillsides to put the road through. Today, the retaining walls that were built to prevent the hills from crumbling onto Sunset are decorated with colorful murals that capture the area's multicultural spirit.

Despite its lyrical-sounding name and fashionable origins, Echo Park for many decades was allowed to decline as residents sought less crowded, noisy, and tattered neighborhoods. As a result, the Echo Park section of Sunset is among the least glamorous stretches—mainly a hardscrabble collection of nuts-and-bolts storefronts and social service agencies, with a few coffee shops, gay bars, antiques emporiums, and restaurants adding touches of color and style. Residents are mostly recent immi-

....

A Red Car bound for Santa Monica travels west on Sunset, passing above automobiles on Glendale Boulevard in 1904. Opposite: An artist's depiction of the same area in "View of East Sunset" (2000) by Suong Yangchareon. The Sunset bridge can be seen in the background.

grants from Mexico, Central America, Cuba, the Philippines, Thailand, and Cambodia, along with various artists and iconoclasts who appreciate the privacy and rustic seclusion of homes built deep into hillsides, invisible from the street yet privy to some of Los Angeles' most breathtaking city views.

In recent years the area's abundance of character-rich older homes has been rediscovered as potentially the last gold mine of affordable real estate in Los Angeles, and the find is sparking a neighborhood transformation. In the 1980s Echo Park hillside homes began to attract downtown professionals weary of long commutes. The area's original sons and daughters, raised in blue-collar environs but now educated and middle-class, also began to snap up houses and see property values rise. So too did a signif-

icant number of gays and lesbians, usually professionals or artists settling down into long-term relationships.

In the 1990s, as the economic boom drove up Westside and suburban home prices, Echo Park's desirability accelerated. A rambling wood bungalow with a view that sold for $150,000 in the mid-1990s was bringing double the price by the end of the century. View streets like Cerro Gordo and lakeside addresses along Echo Park Avenue were suddenly hot properties, all but out of reach of the adventurous urban pioneers of a decade earlier.

Today, this trickling in of wealthier home buyers, along with a growing number of art galleries, antiques shops, and cafes, are nudging working-class, multicultural Echo Park closer in flavor to bohemian and hipster-heavy Silver Lake to the west. Some longtime residents worry that Echo Park will become gentrified, losing its south-of-the-border *sabor* and squeezing out the poor. While that concern ap-

pears unlikely today, the currents of change are clearly at work in these hills and *avenidas* and in the storefronts along Sunset.

A Starry History

With its proximity to downtown, the city's original center, Echo Park has a rich history—one the Echo Park Historical Society is helping to illuminate and preserve. Well-known residents have included evangelist Aimee Semple McPherson, California historian and author Carey McWilliams, bookshop owner and literary salon-maker Jake Zeitlin, artist Ed Ruscha, erotic authoress

Anais Nin, and silent filmmakers and stars such as Mack Sennett, Charlie Chaplin, and Gloria Swanson.

From the silent era onward, moviemaking has been key to the development along Sunset Boulevard. In 1909, comedy innovator Sennett set up shop on a former

··

Above, left: Mack Sennett's Keystone Kops, invented for the movies. Above, right: Actual LAPD officers pose for a 1950 movie photo that captures the era's condescension toward female cops. Opposite, top: Sennett's Keystone studios on Glendale Boulevard, where Chaplin's "Little Tramp" first appeared. Opposite, bottom: Mixville Studios in 1921, established on Teviot Street by cowboy actor Tom Mix.

horse ranch at 1712 Glendale Boulevard, in an area then called Edendale (a designation the local post office still bears).

It was there, in 1914, that Chaplin, a diminutive vaudeville performer from England, first put on a bowler hat and oversized clothes and waddled in front of the cameras as "The Little Tramp." Not sure at first if Chaplin would pull his weight, Sennett was soon paying the comic genius a salary of $1,000 a week—a sum he increased to $10,000 a week the following year. Chaplin went on to worldwide fame and built his own studios further down Sunset, on La Brea Avenue. Also launching careers from the Sennett stable were Swanson, Roscoe

"Fatty" Arbuckle, Carole Lombard, and future filmmaker Frank Capra.

Sennett turned the little Keystone movie studio into a hit-maker. In 1912 he helped birth a bumbling band of frantic cops whose wild escapades were frequently filmed around Echo Park. "Keystone Kops of Echo Park," in fact, was among the many titles. Arbuckle, one of the "Kops," later went on to direct and star in his own films. Swanson, like Lombard employed as one of "Sennett's Bathing Beauties," lived on West Kensington Road overlooking Echo Park Lake. Much later, in 1950, she would become the actress associated around the world with Sunset Boulevard when she performed a gutsy, tragic parody of her own

Greetings from CALIFORNIA

25:—SCENIC BEAUTY IN ECHO PARK. LOS ANGELES. CALIFORNIA.

career in the movie named after the street.

The Sennett Keystone studio was declared a historic landmark in 1982, but today the site is prosaically occupied by a Jack-In-The-Box fast-food restaurant and a Public Storage facility, within which Sennett's concrete soundstage still stands. Down the street, near an off-ramp of the roaring Glendale Freeway, an obelisk with a plaque marks the spot as "the birthplace of motion picture comedy." It's on the grounds of Bert-Co Graphics, which isn't the actual site. There's talk of someday moving the marker down the street to the historic spot, but for now the pilgrimage is a rather dispiriting effort recommended only for true fans.

Another site of historic movie-making importance is 2450 Teviot Street, where movie cowboy Tom Mix once ran his thriving Mixville Studios. Mix began his career working for movie pioneer William Selig, who established Selig Polyscope studios on Glendale Boulevard in 1908, adjacent to the future Sennett site. Mix went on to start his own studio, making 170 Western films, many shot in this area, before he died in a car accident in 1940. McPherson, the evangelist, used to bring her children over to ride horses at Mix's stables on the studio lot.

An Urban Oasis

Echo Park Lake is a true oasis at the city's urban core, redolent of the languid, semitropical ambience associated with romantic visions of a bygone Los Angeles. With its arched red wooden bridge, lotus grove, spouting geysers and curving, palm-fringed paths, the lake is strikingly picturesque and has long been a favorite of filmmakers.

The lake was formed in 1870 when the Canal and Reservoir Company constructed a 20-foot dam to pool water from an underground spring, intending it to be a water supply for the city and a source of power for a nearby woolen mill. After the mill folded, the reservoir and 27 acres of surrounding land were donated to the city in 1891 by their owners, Thomas Kelly and his business partner, Dr. LeMoyne Wills. (Nearby LeMoyne Street is named for the doctor, a noted surgeon and philanthropist who later helped found Childrens Hospital, a few miles farther down Sunset.)

Welcome to Lotus Land

How did Los Angeles come to be referred to as "Lotus Land?" Easterners used the term in reference to the semitropical climate and residents' supposed lack of intellectual rigor. The phrase goes back to Homer's "Odyssey," in which a tribe of people eat the fruit of the lotus tree and experience a dream-like languor and forgetfulness. However, the Egyptian water lily you'll find at Echo Park Lake, which grows mostly in the Nile River and in China, is a different plant than those Homer warned of. The roots of these are edible and, while dried leaves can be smoked, they are not an opiate.

The park was dedicated in 1895. An Englishman named Joseph Henry Tomlinson was named the city's first superintendent of parks, and oversaw the landscaping. The first boathouse, built in 1921, rented wooden canoes. Today's Mission Revival-style boathouse, where fiberglass paddle-board boats rent for $5 a half-hour, was built in the 1930s.

The 15-acre lake, fueled by the underground spring, is the largest in Los Angeles. The geysers at the center were installed to coincide with the 1984 Olympics. From its middle, the lake offers a great view of the neighborhood, including the huge, domed Angelus Temple built in 1923 by world-famous evangelist Aimee Semple McPherson, whose services caused major Sunday night traffic jams in her heyday.

The lake has enjoyed cameo film appearances almost from its creation. The antic silent movies of the Keystone Kops

were filmed here, in the days when Mack Sennett Studios thrived nearby. In *Chinatown*, Jack Nicholson rents a rowboat here to conduct surveillance for a client. Today crews routinely use the signature red bridge, spouting fountain, and lush landscaping as backdrops for films, music videos, and commercials.

Urban surroundings or no, the lake is a popular fishing spot and stocked twice a year. A 20-pound, 2-foot-long carp was once reeled in, if you believe the fish tales of a former park director. Although wading and swimming are prohibited, the lake has claimed several lives, including four in a

• •

Children race model yachts at Echo Park Lake, 1956.

three-year span in the 1930s. One was a suicide; the other victims were listed as drunks. In 1907, after oil from nearby wild-cat drilling operations leaked into the lake, the water actually caught fire and burned for three days.

A huge bed of lotus plants grows in the corner of the lake nearest Angelus Temple, at the intersection of Glendale Boulevard and Park Avenue. While their origin remains a mystery, many believe the story that they were planted by church missionaries returning from China or by Sister Aimee herself. The pink, cinnamon-smelling flowers bloom for several weeks each July, an event marked by a two-day festival that celebrates the Asian and Pacific Island cultures of Echo Park with rides, food, dance, and ceremonies.

On the east shore of the lake near the boathouse stands a 14-foot-tall Art Deco sculpture known as the Lady of the Lake, commissioned in 1934 by the WPA. The stylized female figure watched over the lake for more than 50 years, then fell victim to vandalism and graffiti. In 1999 the piece was restored by the city and the Echo Park Historical Society. Its return is seen by some as symbolic of a neighborhood making a comeback. Still, locals joke that the statue's hands are uplifted in response to a stickup.

At the intersection of Sunset Boulevard and Echo Park Avenue, just north of the lake, stands one of the area's most visible landmarks: Jensen's Recreation Center, with its kitschy lighted sign of a bowler knocking over tenpins. The building, an imposing brick structure that dates to the 1920s, mixes Egyptian elements with the 16th-century Italian renaissance style. Originally a bowling alley and athletic center where athletes like Jackie Robinson put on exhibitions, the structure now contains stores and apartments. The sidewalks on Sunset between Laveta Terrace and Park

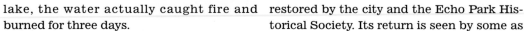

Strikingly elegant bowling alley at Jensen's Recreation Center, 1929.

Avenue feature bronze plaques commemorating athletes who appeared at the center, including Robinson, L.A. Dodgers pitcher Sandy Koufax, and track stars Parry O'Brien and Bob Seagren.

Just east of Alvarado at 1911 Sunset Boulevard is another Echo Park landmark, Taix Restaurant (pronounced "Tex"), serving French country cuisine in Los Angeles since 1927 and at this location since 1962. The Taix family came from the Alps region of southwestern France. The waiters and bartenders count their years of service in decades; some have been there 40 years. Many locals and downtown workers are steady patrons. Evenings, Taix courts a hip, young crowd with offbeat entertainment and an open mike night in the lounge.

Sister Aimee

Since 1923 the huge, domed Angelus Temple at Echo Park Lake has been carrying on the worldwide ministry of the evangelist who built it—a remarkable monument, to be sure. But even more remarkable is the life story of the utterly unusual and gifted person who was its founder, Aimee Semple McPherson.

Born in 1890 to a Canadian farm couple, Aimee Kennedy was promised to the serv-

LA-98— Angelus Temple, Los Angeles, California

Church of the Four Square Gospel

ice of God while still in the womb by her devoutly religious teenage mother. At 17, she married a missionary, Robert Semple, and traveled with him to China. There, her husband contracted dysentery and died, leaving Aimee eight months' pregnant and a widow at age 20. She remarried, bore a second child, and tried to fulfill a housewife's role in the Providence, R.I., hometown of her new husband, Harold McPherson. But she was plagued by massive depression and claims to have heard the insistent voice of God commanding her, "Go! Do the work of an evangelist!"

Tormented by illnesses—perhaps psychosomatic—so severe that she went under the surgeon's knife several times, Aimee was on her deathbed in the hospital when, according to her autobiography, she finally ·swore to answer the call. Overnight, she was healed. Soon after, she bundled up her children and, accompanied by her doting mother, Minnie, slipped away from McPherson. In 1915, this was a shocking departure from social norms, particularly as Harold McPherson had been a blameless husband. But as wretchedly as Aimee had failed under the constraints of marriage, she thrived gloriously in her new role as a saver of souls.

Everywhere she went, the "lady evangel-ist" drew a crowd, offering "that old-time religion" to farm folk who came from hundreds of miles away. She preached her Pentecostal message in a vast tent carried from place to place throughout the United States and Canada. She spoke in tongues. But healing was what really built her legend. The crippled, the blind, the arthritic, the deaf—scores and scores proclaimed instant relief, witnessed by thousands and chronicled in a mountain of newspaper accounts—although Aimee regularly declaimed herself as merely the instrument of a higher power.

The evangelist was thus already famous when she arrived in Los Angeles in Decem-ber 1918, after driving cross-country with her mother and children. Pentecostals in the city were hungry for a leader. The first service, in a hall that seated 700, was mobbed. For the next, Sister Aimee tried a 3,500-seat hall near Pershing Square, only to find every seat taken and long lines forming hours in advance.

She took up residence in a house at 2549 Orange Drive, built by followers who donated services and materials, but Aimee soon hit the road again, drawing crowds of up to 16,000 in major cities, sometimes three times a day. In less than two years, she pulled together a million dollars' worth of cash, donated labor, and

materials to build the Angelus Temple at Echo Park Lake. She oversaw much of the construction herself.

The 5,300-seat auditorium opened on New Year's Day, 1923. Inspired by the thriving nearby Hollywood film industry, Aimee gave broadly funny, theatrical-style services, rich with melodrama and showmanship. The Temple featured a 14-piece orchestra, a 100-voice choir, a 36-piece brass band, and a massive pipe organ.

Once, she had firemen with ladders and a net burst into the crowded theater to "save" a "sinner"—actually a trained acrobat—whom she exhorted to jump from a platform high above the crowd to demonstrate his faith.

Services in Echo Park became a major draw. Tourists could not leave Los Angeles without saying they had witnessed a sermon by Aimee Semple McPherson. On Sunday nights in Echo Park, traffic was so thick that the city scheduled extra Red Car trolleys and assigned special police to move automobiles in and out.

But the spotlight of fame that shone on Aimee so brightly was soon to burn her. On May 18, 1926, she vanished while swimming in the ocean off Venice Beach and was presumed drowned. On June 23—three days after her memorial service—she stumbled into a Mexican border town, dazed and haggard, and told a story of kidnapping, torture, and escape. The newspapers went nuts. Her return by train to Los Angeles drew a crowd of at least 50,000.

Braces and crutches cast off by the evangelist's followers fill a "Miracle Room" at Angelus Temple in the 1930s. Opposite: 1932 opening day of Aimee's Echo Park commissary, which fed thousands during the Depression.

Law enforcement officials, however, were unable to confirm her tale. Aimee's popularity had long irritated the city's Protestant establishment; now, she was accused of perpetuating a hoax and dragged into court to face a grand jury. Rumors circulated that the evangelist had been in Carmel with a married man who worked for her as a radio engineer. District Attorney Asa Keyes hammered away, but Aimee stuck to her story. The government's case eventually fell apart, and she was freed.

But while the prolonged hearing had drawn huge publicity, it had taken a great toll on her health and reputation. Neither ever fully recovered. The scandal had sapped Aimee's ability to draw new followers, and a once-fawning press became increasingly skeptical. She began suffering severe mood swings and was treated for a nervous breakdown in 1930. Her medication became her addiction, and in 1944 she died of a Seconal overdose while on tour in Oakland.

History tends to remember Sister Aimee most vividly for the scandal, but old-time residents of Echo Park remember something else: throughout the Depression years, the evangelist helped tens of thousands of her neighbors survive. The Temple opened a commissary and soup kitchen that gave and gave, distributing food, clothing, and toys. The demand was so great that a second soup kitchen was launched, serving 80,000 people the first month. Aimee also persuaded the federal government to open an abandoned Army building so 25,000 jobless people could be housed.

The late Anthony Quinn, who lived near the Angelus Temple as a youth, in a tiny house with his widowed mother and ailing grandmother, recalled in a national television interview how Aimee helped him when he was "literally fainting on the street from hunger." The future acting great later began to play saxophone in the church's band, and accompanied Sister Aimee into East L.A. to translate her sermons into Spanish from the stage of a tent revival.

More than 75 years later, Aimee's Temple is a National Historic Landmark and her Church of the Foursquare Gospel is a 3.3-million-member organization active in 107 countries.

A Victorian Pocket

Angelino Heights, one of Los Angeles' most unusual and historic neighborhoods, is located in Echo Park just south of Sunset Boulevard. Its heart is in the 1300 block of Carroll Avenue—a peaceful, breeze-cooled hilltop where turn-of-the-century gingerbread houses contrast with a startling view of the contemporary downtown skyline.

Most of these ornately restored Victorian landmarks were constructed between the 1880s and 1900 in response to the population boom fed by the newly arriving transcontinental railway. Angelino Heights was laid out conveniently to downtown in 1886 by developers William Stilson and Everett Hall, who held interests in a cable car company serving the central city. The location was meant to appeal to the well-to-do, who typically spent the then-considerable sum of $5,000 to $10,000 to build their extravagant homes, mostly in the Queen Anne–Eastlake and Carpenter Gothic styles.

The subdivision fronted on Bellevue Avenue, where streetcars appeared at 10-minute intervals and made the run to downtown's Spring Street in 16 minutes. Angelino Heights became L.A.'s first real suburb—the "in spot" for wealthy bankers, businessmen, and socialites who mingled in the ballrooms of mansions in the tony residential enclave.

But as times changed, Los Angeles spread outward and downtown addresses became unfashionable. The grand houses—including beauties on surrounding thoroughfares such as Kellam Avenue, Kensington Road, Bellevue Avenue, Edgeware Road, and Douglas Street—fell into neglect for decades until the 1970s, when a movement took hold among urban pioneers and preservationists to restore them. One couple, Murray Burns and Planaria Price, have

restored more than 16 residences on the hill. In the 1300 block of Carroll Avenue, 17 homes have been designated historic and cultural monuments by the Los Angeles Cultural Heritage Commission. In 1975, the Carroll Avenue Restoration Foundation was formed and succeeded in getting the

A Victorian home on Carroll Avenue today, looking much the same as in 1900. Opposite: A painting of Carroll Avenue in 1976, by artist Leo Politi.

city to name Angelino Heights L.A.'s first historic preservation zone. The group also raised funds to install vintage streetlights.

Today, the hill looms large at Halloween for children in surrounding neighborhoods, who descend en masse to beg treats at the high, ancient abodes that transform marvelously into haunted houses. The area is used frequently in filming, and is a favorite of tourists and visitors, including downtown workers who zip through on their lunch hours for brief immersions in another era. On the first Saturday of each month, the Los Angeles Conservancy offers guided tours of Angelino Heights Carroll Avenue, including entry into selected homes with authentic period decor.

Elysian Park

Located north of Sunset Boulevard within Echo Park, Elysian Park contains more than 500 acres of meadows, trails and bike paths in what is the city's oldest public parkland. Some of the steepest streets in California are found in the surrounding residential neighborhoods. In the early 1900s, outdoor stairways were built so residents could reach their houses. A horse-drawn trolley, the Elysian Park Railway, dropped

Mean Streets

The alpine streets of Echo Park and Silver Lake offer a heart-pounding, bun-tightening workout for walkers and a do-or-die challenge for aging automobiles. Fargo Street is the steepest in California, with a 32 percent grade in the section that climbs the hills northeast of the Glendale Freeway. Nearby Baxter, Cerro Gordo, and Duane streets are not quite as steep, but still inspire fear and disbelief in motorists—and still beat anything in the Bay Area. Members of a local bicycle club, the Los Angeles Wheelmen, have gathered at the foot of Fargo Street each spring since 1972 to test their mettle by attempting to pedal it.

off locals at the stairway nearest their homes.

Elysian Park also contains Dodger Stadium—a story in itself—and the Los Angeles Police Academy, the primary training facility of the LAPD. The academy, in the hills above Sunset near Dodger Stadium, is open to the public. The campus, with its shooting range and classrooms, has a surprisingly laid-back, Mediterranean feel thanks to Spanish-style buildings; an outdoor, Olympic-size swimming pool; and a Polynesian-style terraced rock garden.

The land was first used in 1926 as a makeshift shooting range, then upgraded for use in the 1932 Olympics. In 1934, then-Police Chief James Davis decided to build a training academy and raised most of the money from private sources. The first class graduated in 1936. There are additional campuses today, but the site remains the primary training facility for the LAPD. Visitors who arrive at the right time can use an observation deck to watch trainees on the shooting range.

Landscape architect Francois Scotti had the rock garden built into a hillside in 1937. Used for weddings and parties—presumably law-abiding ones—the huge layout includes four terraced pools with cascades, tropical foliage, and big Flintstones-style rocks; a dining area; an amphitheater; and trails that lead off in intriguing private directions.

There's no museum on campus, but the walls of the Los Angeles Police Revolver and Athletic Club Cafe, open to the public for breakfast and lunch, are full of historic photos. This is the place to rub elbows with all manner of law enforcement officers, including the "uniforms," who hang their hats on pegs on the back of the chairs. The campus gift store is also popular with visitors. Here, police fetishists can buy LAPD everything, from T-shirts, caps, and mugs to uniform gear and even weapons.

From Chavez Ravine to Dodger Stadium

Just off Sunset up Elysian Park Boulevard is Dodger Stadium, L.A.'s temple to baseball since 1962, when it was built as a home for the team imported from Brooklyn. With a lush setting against the hills of Chavez Ravine, a symmetrical, open-bowl design, and 56,000 cantilevered seats, it's a beauty of a ballpark, given extra pizzazz in a $50-million renovation completed before the 2000 season.

But there's another story here—one that's literally beneath the feet of fans as they tread the parking lot. It's the story of the settlement of working-class immigrants, mostly from Mexico, that thrived in the steep-sided ravine from the 1920s through the 1950s.

Many in Los Angeles believe that community was destroyed when the city conspired with Brooklyn Dodgers owner Walter O'Malley to bring the ball team to L.A. The real story, however, is richer and more interesting.

The dismantling of Chavez Ravine actually began through the efforts of well-meaning social reformers. In 1946, after a study by the city planning commission cited substandard housing and declared the neighborhood a blighted area, the city decided to tear it down and replace it with a federal housing project. No less an architect than Richard Neutra, the acclaimed Modernist, was hired. Under Neutra's direction, plans were drawn and models were built for an extensive village to be called Elysian Park Heights, comprised of 163 two-story buildings and two dozen 13-story towers, with up-to-date plumbing, electricity, and telephone lines.

Residents of Chavez Ravine were informed of the plan in July 1950, via letters from the city informing them they had to relocate. The city intended to appraise their dwellings and offer them a price. When the new units were ready, they could return and have first choice, with rents to

Opposite: Dodger Stadium being constructed, 1960.

be based on income.

Absentee landlords began to sell the houses out from under their tenants. Even home-owning residents sold out. And so began the demise of Chavez Ravine. Over the next few years, the population dwindled from about 200 families to about 20.

But political currents were rising that would doom the federal housing project and leave the former residents of Chavez Ravine with only broken promises. Senator Joseph McCarthy had launched his campaign against the so-called Communist infiltration of the U.S. government in February 1950. Foes of the Chavez Ravine housing plan began to denounce it as "creeping socialism," and in 1953 Los Angeles voters replaced Fletcher Bowron, the mayor who favored federal housing projects, with Norris Poulson, who opposed them.

Poulson killed the housing project right after he took office. Los Angeles voters backed him up. In a referendum election, 600,000 citizens voted three to two to abandon the projects. This action, usurping a federal investment, was highly questionable. But California's two members of the U.S. Senate, Richard M. Nixon and William F. Knowland, successfully pushed for federal legislation to validate the city's action.

For the families that had held out in Chavez Ravine, all this might have been good news, but it was too late. Already, empty dwellings had been set ablaze by the fire department during training exercises for new recruits. Other structures had fallen to ruin or been carted away, brick by brick.

By mid-1953, the housing authority was beaten, and it sold Chavez Ravine back to the city of Los Angeles at a substantial loss to the federal government. Congress then decreed that the land had to be used for

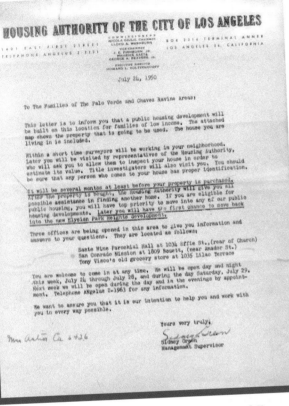

public purposes, but Mayor Poulson had other ideas.

This is when the Dodgers entered the picture. Los Angeles was finally in a position to get its own major league baseball team, partly because improved airplane

······················

Above: Letter sent to Chavez Ravine residents informing them their homes would be appraised and purchased out from under them. Right: Evictions took place on live television in May 1959. Opposite: 1952 artist's sketch of modern housing project that was promised to residents and later abandoned.

travel had made access to the West Coast easier in a major league circuit dominated by East Coast and Midwest teams. At the same time, Brooklyn Dodgers owner Walter O'Malley was having trouble negotiating a new stadium site with the city of New York.

Poulson and his cronies offered Chavez Ravine to O'Malley on very favorable terms. The city council knew this was against the rules, so a referendum election was held to gain public support. Amid outrage and controversy, voters approved the Dodger deal by a margin of less than two percent. But there was more to come. A Superior Court judge found the council's action "an abdication of public trust and a gross abuse of discretion." But a judge on the California Supreme Court ruled otherwise. The Dodgers were in.

Now came time for the city to evict the remaining residents. One family, the Arechigas, had lived in their home since 1923. They had hissed at their neigh-

bors for selling and they had watched while other houses were burned, buried, or carted away. They weren't leaving.

In May of 1959, county sheriffs came in to do the job, and television crews came with them. The deputies kicked in the door of the Arechiga home and carried four struggling women down the stairs. A bulldozer then mowed the home into matchsticks. The drama of this live confrontation —broadcast across the nation—outraged many viewers. Letters expressing shock and disgust poured in. But the city prevailed. The promises made to residents dissolved in the tides of history. A baseball

blare the voice of announcer Vin Scully. Stadium lights cast a glow in the sky, and on featured nights fireworks burst over the scene, visible for miles around.

Former residents of Chavez Ravine and their descendants are some of the Dodgers' most loyal fans. But once a year, they gather for a picnic in Elysian Park—the one area where the promise of public use was maintained—to reminisce about a simpler time when the music of Mexican balladeers wafted through these hills.

The story of those days is beautifully documented in words and pictures by photographer Don Normark in his book *Chavez Ravine 1949: A Los Angeles Story*. Through the recollections of former residents, Normark's book evokes a neighborhood of hundreds of homes built up and down the hills, some solid, two-story frame houses with wide porches, others tumble-down shacks with

stadium went up where their tidy, modern, subsidized homes were supposed to be.

Construction on privately financed Dodger Stadium began September 17, 1959. The steep terrain was reshaped—more than eight million cubic yards of earth were moved—and 21,000 pre-cast concrete forms weighing up to 32 tons each were lifted into

place to comprise the stadium's structural framework. Opening day was April 2, 1962, and the stadium drew 2.7 million ticket buyers in its first year.

Today, during at least 60 night games a year, the once-quiet hills of Chavez Ravine draw swarms of traffic. Ticket scalpers wave their wares at cars along Sunset and radios

••••••••••••••••••••

Dodger fans in nosebleed section, 1998. Opposite: Palo Verde schoolyard, later buried under ballpark.

Check it out: Echo Park

Food and Drink

Short Stop, 1455 Sunset Boulevard, (213) 482-4942. Former LAPD watering hole, now a hipster hang with billiards.

Barragan's, 1538 Sunset Boulevard, (213) 250-4256. Casual, friendly, decades-old Mexican place. Great margaritas, Friday happy hour buffet.

Taix Restaurant, 1911 Sunset Boulevard, (213) 484-1265. Local institution serving French country cuisine.

El Carmelo Bakery, 1800 Sunset Boulevard, (213) 483-4748. Pastries, Cuban coffee.

Downbeat Cafe, 1202 Alvarado Street (at Sunset), (213) 483-3955. Upbeat, arty hang serving espresso, salads, sandwiches.

LAPD Revolver and Athletic Club Cafe, 1880 Academy Road (at the Police Academy), (323) 221-5222. Breakfast, lunch alongside police trainees til 2 p.m. daily.

Art Scene

Gallery Row, including art and photo galleries Ojala, Fototeka, Delirium Tremens, and Pink, located 1547-1555 Echo Park Avenue, two blocks north of Sunset. Regular events and simultaneous openings. Information: (213) 250-4686.

Specialty Shopping

Antique Row, (2200 block of Sunset, between Mohawk and Rosemont, both sides of street). Intriguing row of shops with rich, eclectic collections of antiques, Americana, tiles, and pottery, comprised of Wells Antiques, Again L.A., Peron Collectibles, Minnette's, and other shops.

Book Bound, 1545 Echo Park Avenue (in Gallery Row), (213) 481-0802. Smart, sassy bookstore with local focus.

Special Events

Lotus Festival. Annual event held early to mid-July at Echo Park Lake, coincides with brief blooming of floating lotus grove. Celebrates Asian-Pacific culture with ceremonies, dance, music, food. Information: (213) 485-1310.

Echo Park Arts Festival. Annual event held mid-October, featuring artists' studio tours, historic tours, crafts and art, children's activities. Information: (213) 250-4155.

Echo Park History Day (at Barlow Sanitarium in Elysian Park). Annual open house held at the historic hospice in Elysian Park (built in 1902 for treatment of tuberculosis) features speeches, tours, vintage photos and memorabilia, and oral history sessions with Echo Park old-timers. Date varies. Information: Echo Park Historical Society, (323) 860-8874.

tin roofs and no plumbing or electricity. There were few telephones. Children flew down the steep hills on homemade carts. Goats and sheep grazed on the hillsides.

Residents remember the Santo Niño Catholic Church, where Father Thomas presided over baptisms, weddings, confirmations, and funerals. They recall the small stores, some of which extended credit to cash-strapped residents. And they can never forget Palo Verde Elemen-

tary School, where generations of children, some attending classes in bare feet, learned to speak English.

When the settlement was bulldozed, the roof of the school was removed so it could be filled in with earth. The Palo Verde school still remains down there, beneath the parking lot of Dodger Stadium. ⓢ

Silver Lake

Los Feliz

Franklin

Hollywood

Hillhurst

Sunset

Fountain

Santa Monica

Virgil

Hoover

Hyperion

Griffith Park

Silver Lake Reservoir

Micheltorena

Silver Lake

Coronado

Alvarado

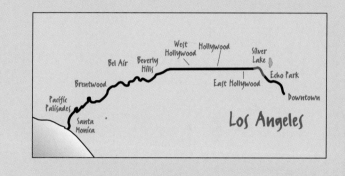

Los Angeles

Pacific Palisades · Santa Monica · Brentwood · Bel Air · Beverly Hills · West Hollywood · Hollywood · East Hollywood · Silver Lake · Echo Park · Downtown

① Sunset Junction

② Epitaph Records/site of the Olive Street Substation

③ The Silver Lake Bridge

④ Original Site of Disney Studios

⑤ The Music Box Steps

⑥ The Paramour/The Moreno Mansion

⑦ Silvertop

⑧ Group of Neutra-designed homes

Opposite: Looking northeast over Silver Lake in 1926. Sunset Boulevard is the first major east-west thoroughfare south of the reservoir, in the approximate center of the photograph.

Magician Christopher Wonder poses with his wife and assistant, Marlo, in the rabbit-themed bathroom of their Silver Lake home. Opposite, left: Millie's is an old and popular restaurant on the boulevard. Opposite, right: The Snivling Sibbling bills itself as a "vintage department store."

Silver Lake, an authentically edgy urban

enclave exhibiting both today's social ills and a maverick
artistic spirit, is ground zero for the Eastside versus Westside
lifestyle debate. Its sidewalks and outdoor cafe tables are
trafficked by a remarkably high concentration of creative

folk—part of a population at least half Latino, with a full-on mix of the gay and the straight, the working class and the white-collar. Silver Lake is a neighborhood where diversity is put to its greatest test and fosters, in return, a stronger sense of community.

For all those living *la vida loca* in the streets, clubs, and studios, there are as many living *la vida tranquilla*. Silver Lake's densely packed hillsides—which include some classic Modernist homes—are inhabited largely by middle-class families and professionals, and these sections are remarkably peaceful, given their

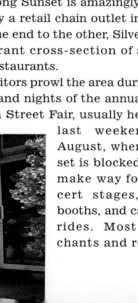

proximity to the urban grind. The neighborhood's popular coffee shop culture was only recently invaded by a Starbuck's. The shopping along Sunset is amazingly eclectic, with nary a retail chain outlet in sight. And, from one end to the other, Silver Lake offers a vibrant cross-section of shops, cafes, and restaurants.

Many visitors prowl the area during the hectic days and nights of the annual Sunset Junction Street Fair, usually held the last weekend in August, when Sunset is blocked off to make way for concert stages, food booths, and carnival rides. Most merchants and restaurants stay open to take advantage of the influx. The event was launched in 1980 to bridge tensions between gays and gang members, and has become a no-holds-barred parade of diversity, as transvestites strut their stuff alongside teenage ravers

and immigrant families with children. The festival helps fund the Tsunami Coffeehouse at Sunset Junction, which offers city-subsidized jobs and counseling for area youth.

In exploring the area on foot, perhaps the best place to begin is at "Sunset junction" itself, where Sanborn Street, Santa Monica Boulevard, and Sunset intersect. Within steps, you'll find the French-Moroccan Cafe Casbah and adjacent Snivling Sibbling, an eclectic antiques shop. Among the boulevard's more historic eateries is Millie's, serving locals since the 1920s. Back then, it was called the Devil's Mess. There's still a breakfast dish on the menu with this name. Nowadays, the counter and 25-seat eatery is known for strong coffee, great biscuits, good food, and plenty of personality and attitude from the tattooed hash-slingers, many of

whom play in rock bands by night.

While funky, vibrant Sunset Boulevard is its main drag, the community's natural focus is Silver Lake Reservoir, on Silver Lake Boulevard about a half-mile north of Sunset. Cradled beneath the neighborhood's steep hills and offering panoramic views of the Griffith Observatory, the Hollywood sign, and the purple San Bernardino mountains, the lake offers a tranquil respite in the middle of an otherwise crowded urban core. These are the sparkling turquoise waters for which many understandably—but erroneously—believe the area was named. Actually, the reservoir, built in 1906 as part of Los Angeles' municipal water supply devised by William Mulholland, was named after Herman Silver,

a former water commissioner and city council president.

Houses with views of the water are much prized, and some exceptional examples of Modernist architecture surround the lake. An excellent lake view can be had from the bell tower on Cove Avenue, off Silver Lake Boulevard, by those willing to join the workout enthusiasts who regularly

climb the 154 steps leading to it.

A crisis arose in the late 1980s when the city's Department of Water and Power devised a plan to cover up the reservoir with plastic or aluminum, citing concerns about maintaining water purity. Beginning in 1988, residents mobilized to fight the proposal and they prevailed. Silver Lake is now

Sunset near the junction with Micheltorena in 1909. Opposite, top: Looking northwest over Silver Lake Reservoir. Opposite, bottom: Carving out Sunset in 1909 at the Coronado Grade as the boulevard enters Silver Lake.

a city historical monument, and the water department has approved a plan to replace the rather grim fence surrounding the reservoir's two-and-a-quarter-mile perimeter and to open some of its grassy surroundings to walkers and runners.

Silver Lake Park, at the southwest corner of the lake, offers a pocket of tranquility with a recreation center and nearby dog park. Also nearby are the popular Back Door Bakery, where locals linger over cappuccino the live-long day, and Netty's, where fine food is ordered counter-style and brought to the outside patio.

The Music Scene

Musicians have been occupying cheap Silver Lake digs for decades, but the scene really caught fire in 1993, when a song called "Loser" burst onto alternative radio and became the overnight anthem for the slacker generation.

Twenty-three-year-old native son Beck Hansen, then a skinny, shambling Silver Lake resident, had recorded the tune on a no-budget indie label, Bong Load. His first album, *Mellow Gold*, teemed with site-specific creativity, combining Dylanesque lyrics with Spanish phrases and inner-city hip-hop rhythms, country elements and a unique, desultory vocal delivery. Beck was hailed in the music press as the voice of a generation, and Silver Lake became the place to be for aspiring alternative-rock musicians.

With his thrift-store wardrobe and genius head for music, Beck and his collage of influences seemed to sum up funky, multiethnic Silver Lake. His 1996 followup album, *Odelay*, recorded with Silver Lake-based producers the Dust Brothers, was one of the most critically acclaimed and influential records of the year.

Although Beck moved out of Silver

Beastie Boys. The loose-knit "Eastside scene" has also been home to critics' favorites the Negro Problem and lead singer Stew, along with the Geraldine Fibbers, Extra Fancy, roots rocker Dave Alvin, Concrete Blonde, and X, the seminal Los Angeles punk rock band of the 1980s. (Various Eastside bands are documented on the 1996 compilation album *Silver Lake…What A Drag!* on Neurotic Records.)

Silver Lake's music scene intersects with its early-day history at the corner of Sunset and Occidental boulevards, where a former Red Car trolley station has been turned into the headquarters of indie music label Epitaph Records. Once known as the Olive Street substation, the elegant, ivy-covered brick building has stood since at least 1920. Streetcars entered at the arched doorway on Sunset, were spun around on a rotary platform, and left the station going the other direction.

Retired from service, the station served as an architect's office before Bad Religion guitarist Brett Gurewitz leased it in 1990 as headquarters for a new record label. Epitaph rocked the music industry when it sold

eight million copies of the album *Smash* by Orange County-based band Offspring. Its roster now includes Tom Waits and Merle Haggard as well as Rancid, Pennywise, Buju Banton, and the Voodoo Glow Skulls.

Below the Silver Lake bridge (where Sunset crosses Silver Lake Boulevard) lies testament to the neighborhood's musical flavor—a mural commemorating the hit song "Under the Bridge" by local rock

Lake and went on to international stardom, the Dust Brothers, composed of John King and Mike Simpson, became famed for their cutting-edge approach to digital sampling, created in a Mac-based studio in a Silver Lake house. There, they also mixed the milestone album *Paul's Boutique* for the

heroes the Red Hot Chili Peppers. From the Chili Peppers' breakout album *Love Sugar Sex Magik*, the song is a haunting valentine to the City of Angels and a junkie's lament.

The 100-foot mural, dedicated "to the musicians and artists of Silver Lake," was co-commissioned in 1994 by the band, after losing guitarist Hillel Slovak to an overdose, and Johnette Napolitano, lead singer of Concrete Blonde, who at the time was running a now-closed Silver Lake art gallery, the Lucky Nun. The artist was Ernesto de la Loza, one of the pioneers of the East Los Angeles mural movement. Its image of racehorses running from a tsunami wave, he said, is meant to illustrate how the pressures of city life threaten to overwhelm people and contribute to drug use. The bridge itself, built in 1934, is distinctive for its eight Romanesque brick arches, and has been designated a historic landmark by the city.

••••••••••••••••••••••••••••

Detail of mural on Silver Lake Boulevard under the Sunset Bridge, shown above, circa the 1930s. Opposite, clockwise from far left: Beck Hansen performs at the El Rey Theatre in 1997. The Pacific Electric substation in 1909; the building, at Sunset and Occidental boulevards, is now home to Epitaph Records. The Delphines play at the Garage in 1998.

Listen Up!

Live Music Venues

Spaceland, 1717 Silver Lake Boulevard, (323) 661-4380. Alternative rock and pop. Owner Mitchell Frank also co-owns Nickelbag Records with the Dust Brothers. Beck, Elliot Smith, Grant Lee Buffalo, Pavement, and Mary Lou Lords have appeared.

The Garage, 4519 Santa Monica Boulevard, (323) 662-6802. Hard-core rock and pop and themed club nights.

Dragstrip 66 at Rudolpho's, 2500 Riverside Drive, (323) 669-1226. Popular monthly drag club theme night at a Mexican restaurant.

Silverlake Lounge, 2906 Sunset Boulevard, (323) 666-2407. Bar with weekend drag shows.

Record Stores

Rockaway Records, 2395 Glendale Boulevard, (323) 664-3232.

Destroy All Music, 3818 Sunset Boulevard, (323) 663-9300.

Silver Lake in Film

Silver Lake, Echo Park, and neighboring
East Hollywood were all important areas in
the early development of L.A.'s film history.
That heritage is commemorated in the
annual Silver Lake Film Festival, launched
in September 2000 and dedicated to bringing together the filmmakers, artists, and
craftspeople of the area.

In the heart of Silver Lake, about a mile
off Sunset on Hyperion Avenue, is the site of
the original Walt Disney Studios where
Mickey Mouse and Snow White were created. A plaque on the side of the Mayfair Market marks the spot, and a cluster of very
Disney-esque cottages still stands on Griffith Park Boulevard nearby.

Just south of Sunset on Vendome
Street, across from a small "pocket" park,
movie buffs can visit the steep stairway
(at 923-925 Vendome) used in the movie
The Music Box. In 1932, comedians Stan
Laurel and Oliver Hardy, working for producer Hal Roach, gazed at the staircase
and hatched the idea for the beloved
comic caper, which won a short film Academy Award. In the movie, they pose as
piano movers who tackle the Sisyphean
task of moving a crated piano up the 133

steps that connect Vendome and Descanso Drive. The box keeps tumbling down, until the hapless movers finally reach the

....

The Selig Studios used Silver Lake Reservoir during shooting of *The Roman* in 1909. Opposite: Filming *The Music Box* with Laurel and Hardy in 1932. The steps have since been named to commemorate the movie.

top, only to be informed by the postman that they could have simply driven around to the top!

A 16mm print of *The Music Box* is shown each September at a festival for children at the park across from the steps. The black-and-white movie is projected in a tent, and the presence of Laurel and

Hardy lookalikes and vintage autos adds to the fun.

Visiting the stairway has become something of a pilgrimage for lovers of Laurel and Hardy, and there are many. Ray Bradbury's short story, "The Laurel & Hardy Love Affair," describes lovers who meet at the steps and often picnic there. In an unpublished story called "Another Fine Mess," Bradbury writes about a woman who hears the ghosts of Laurel and Hardy running up and down the steps in the middle of the nights, and hears a piano crate tumbling repeatedly down.

North of Sunset at Micheltorena Street are other historic sites. One is the modest bungalow with a rooftop music studio at 1734 Micheltorena, once the gathering spot for an extraordinary group of classical and experimental musicians during the genesis of the "Evenings on the Roof" concert series. The studio, still visible from the street, was designed by Rudolph Schindler for concert pianist Frances Mullen and her

husband, Peter Yates, a passionate supporter of serious music who decided to create a space where important new works
could be heard.

A civil servant by day, Yates devoted his
nights to corresponding with musicians and
composers to build up the series. Before
long, talents like Arnold Schoenberg and
Igor Stravinsky, pianist Arthur Rubinstein,
violinists Joseph Szigeti and Jascha Heifetz,
and L.A. Philharmonic conductor Otto
Klemperer were trekking up the hill and
crowding into the tiny space to hear performances. The first concert was April 23,
1939, and drew 19 people to hear a program
of Bartok. Tickets were 50 cents and provided the musicians' only wages. The series
quickly outgrew the rooftop and moved to
larger venues. Yates retired from running it
in 1954, but more than 60 years after its
debut, the series continues as the Monday
Evening Concerts at the Bing Theater at the
Los Angeles County Museum of Art.

Farther up Micheltorena, at the crest of
the hill, is a remarkable walled residence that
silent film buffs know as the former home of
heartthrob Antonio Moreno. The Moreno
Mansion, or the Paramour, as it's now called,
is also the place where modern-day
heartthrob Leonardo DiCaprio threw his mil-

lennial New Year's Eve bash. Moreno started
the party tradition back in the 1920s, when
he and his heiress wife, Daisy Canfield, hosted famous guests such as Buster Keaton,
Norma Shearer, and Tom Mix around the
hand-tiled swimming pool of the five-acre

estate, which enjoys a 360-degree
view of Silver Lake and environs.
The 22-room Mediterranean-
style house was designed by
Robert Farquhar, architect of the
California Club in downtown Los
Angeles and of the Pentagon in
Washington, D.C.

Purchased by the couple
with Canfield oil money, the
Moreno Mansion is linked to a
chilling bit of early Los Angeles
mayhem.

In 1906, Daisy's mother,
beloved socialite Chloe P. Canfield, was shot to death by a former family employee after refusing to make him a loan. Chloe's
husband, Charles A. Canfield,
was a partner of Edward L.
Doheny. The two became among
the city's most wealthy and
prominent businessmen after
ushering in the Los Angeles oil
industry with their gusher at Crown Hill
northwest of downtown in 1882, the city's

••••••••••••••••••••

Antonio Moreno and Daisy Canfield at their Silver Lake
estate, now known as the Paramour. Opposite: Walt Disney (right) consults with animators of *Peter Pan* in 1952.

first. Although Chloe's killer was captured and later executed at San Quentin, Charles Canfield never recovered from the shock and grief and died a widower in 1913.

In 1923, Daisy married silent film star Antonio Moreno, a much-in-demand Latin lover-style actor who had starred with Gloria Swanson in the first picture ever shown at Grauman's Chinese Theatre, *My American Wife*, in 1922. But their happiness was short-lived. The couple separated in 1933 and Daisy died a few weeks later while racing along Mulholland Drive with a friend, who drove her car over a 300-foot cliff. Moreno never remarried and died at age 80 in 1967.

The mansion the couple had turned into a party palace for a few fun-filled years became the Chloe P. Canfield Memorial Home for girls after the couple moved out in 1929. From there, it became a residence for Franciscan nuns. After the 1994 earthquake, the structure sat empty for years because of damage. It recently passed into private hands and is now rented for movie shoots, private parties, and other events.

The Silver Lake Film Festival held its closing night party at the mansion in 2000 and 2001, each time showing one of Moreno's silent movies on a giant screen set up on the lawn.

Disney's First Home

You wouldn't know it to look around now, but Mickey Mouse and the Disney empire were born in the heart of Silver Lake.

In 1926, young cartoonist and entrepreneur Walt Disney and his brother Roy moved their fledgling cartooning enterprise into a simple, one-story studio at 2719 Hyperion Avenue, where the Mayfair Market now stands across from Trader Joe's.

They hung out a shingle identifying it as Walt Disney Studios and hired about a dozen animators, inkers, and painters, who often broke off work for a noontime baseball game in the vacant lot across the street, sometimes joined by Walt for an inning or two. Walt and Roy even built adjoining homes on nearby Lyric Avenue, where Walt sometimes worked on animation projects in his garage.

Disney's most famous

character, Mickey Mouse, was created in 1928 by Walt and animated by his partner, Ub Iwerks. Mickey's debut in *Steamboat Willie* was an immediate hit and showcased the studio's ability to master the relatively new art of sound in movies. Mickey's high-pitched voice and the film's clever sound effects, all technologies developed on Hyperion, were considered especially innovative for the day.

Steamboat Willie propelled Disney animation to a new level of success. A series of Mickey Mouse cartoons was followed by *The Three Little Pigs*. Quality was Walt's hallmark. By 1933, the Hyperion facility had expanded to encompass various buildings and a staff of 187. A full-time art school was established on site. Students, including many of the animators who would shape the industry, often traipsed over to Griffith Park Zoo to sketch the animals.

In 1934, Walt hatched plans for the first full-length animated feature. At the Hyperion studio, he gave a two-hour performance for his staff, acting out each character in *Snow White and the Seven Dwarfs*, including the wicked Queen. Although derided by competitors as "Disney's Folly" for its unheard-of $1.5-million production cost, *Snow White* became a smash hit, grossing $8 million worldwide (when ticket prices averaged 23 cents for adults and 10 cents for children) and redrawing the possibilities for the animation industry.

Disney went on to supervise *Fantasia* and parts of *Bambi* on the Hyperion lot before the cramped quarters had to give way to a spacious new studio in Burbank. On the day after Christmas in 1938, most of the staff began the move. A new feature, *Pinocchio*, began filming on the Burbank lot in August 1939, and the Silver Lake era was a wrap.

Gay Silver Lake

Beginning in the late 1960s, the Silver Lake area became increasingly popular with the gay community. A cluster of low-key beer-and-billiards bars, aimed at a gay clientele, established itself along Sunset Boulevard, and the neighborhood's historic embrace of diversity—along with the privacy of houses tucked into its leafy hillsides—inspired many gay couples to settle there.

But Silver Lake didn't offer complete insulation from the era's intolerance. Constant police harassment was a fact of gay life. One notorious incident took place at the Black Cat Bar at 3909 Sunset Boulevard (where the gay bar Le Barcito now stands) on New Year's Eve, 1967. Patrons, many dressed in drag, were attacked by undercover vice cops after some exchanged kisses at the stroke of midnight. The cops dealt out brutal beatings and made more than a dozen arrests. The melee continued at an adjacent Silver Lake nightspot, New Faces, where police billy clubs put a bartender in the hospital for more than a week.

••••••••••••••••••••••

Disney's first studio on Hyperion Avenue is now a supermarket. Opposite: Boys dress up as schoolgirls at a Dragstrip 66 party at Rudolpho's in 1998.

The resulting outrage led to L.A.'s first public demonstration in favor of gay rights and against "police lawlessness," on Sunset in front of the Black Cat on February 11, 1968. Thousands of leaflets were distributed but only about 200 gay men dared march, protected by the presence of several attorneys and clergymen who rather boldly took up their cause. (L.A's first real gay pride parade would take place in nearby East Hollywood two years later, when about 1,800 people marched down Holly-wood Boulevard in June 1970 on the first anniversary of the Stonewall rebellion in New York.)

In 1971, the city's first gay women's center was founded in Silver Lake at 1168 Glendale Boulevard with the goal of creating a supportive and enlightened community. It persisted for more than a year before foundering for lack of funding.

As more gay residents moved in, an increasingly "out" scene began to develop. L.A.'s first gay bookstore, A Different Light, opened in the summer of 1979 in Silver Lake at the corner of Sunset and Santa Monica. It quickly became a center of gay and lesbian cultural life, dispensing information unavailable elsewhere and featuring readings by writers such as John Rechy, whose *City of Night* and *Numbers* explored rituals of gay life in L.A., particularly the notorious 1970s cruising scene in nearby Griffith Park.

In the 1980s, West Hollywood developed an increasingly open and empowered gay community. A Different Light followed that trend, moving into the heart of the action at 8853 Santa Monica Boulevard and closing its Silver Lake store in 1992.

One notorious gay outpost in Silver Lake, an elaborate bath house at 2801 Hyperion Avenue called the Men's Action Center (MAC), was ordered closed down in 1988 by a superior court judge concerned about the AIDS crisis.

Today the influence of gay residents is pervasive, from Silver Lake politics to culture to real estate and the local economy. Many of the businesses that make the Sunset Boulevard commercial strip so attractive and inventive are gay owned and operated.

This relaxed integration of lifestyles is an achievement celebrated each year at the Sunset Junction Street Fair. And nobody blinked when more males than females entered the first-ever "Queen of Silver Lake" contest sponsored by the community's Chamber of Commerce in 2001, although a woman did win the crown. Proceeds benefited an AIDS-related local charity, the Alegria House.

A Modernist Tradition

Silver Lake is home to a high concentration of historic houses by such Modernist architects as Rudolph Schindler, Richard Neutra, Gregory Ain, and John Lautner. In fact, architectural historian Ted Wells says more of these signature homes exist in Silver Lake than in any other neighborhood in the world.

Why? Wells says that at the time these architects were interested in experimenting with their bold, new approaches to home design in the mid-1900s, Silver Lake offered many of the right conditions. Hillside lots, with unique architectural challenges and opportunities to exploit expansive vistas, were still relatively inexpensive in Silver Lake. And educated and creative homebuyers, the ideal clients for such experimental homes, were drawn to the neighborhood because of its diversity and cultural openness.

The Modernists took full advantage of the Southern California climate and Silver Lake's dazzling water and mountain views to create houses that achieved a stunning

meld of indoor and outdoor environments, and a remarkable blend of openness and privacy. Glass walls, some with seemingly invisible mitered corners, allowed residents to feel they were outdoors even in the comfort of their homes. Spatial innovation and the imaginative use of inexpensive or unconventional building materials, other hallmarks of Modernism, gave the homes an approachable, informal feeling. And, outfitted with sleek kitchens and utilitarian touches, the homes presaged a space-age, Jetsons-like existence.

The area's best known and most celebrated home is the spacious hilltop showplace known as Silvertop (2138 Micheltorena Street), designed by Lautner and constructed over the course of 1957 to 1964. The dramatic house features a 12-foot sliding glass panel with a stunning water view and the world's first "infinity" swimming pool,

which appears to overflow and blend with the reservoir.

Directly across the reservoir, at 2300 Silver Lake Boulevard, is the family home built by Neutra in the 1930s, then rebuilt and amended by son Dion after a devastating fire in the 1960s. Known as the VDL Research House, it is owned by the design school at California State Polytechnic University, Pomona. The structure uses light, water, and air as design elements to achieve the contemplative feel that made it an ideal studio environment for Neutra and disciple Ain, who worked alongside him there in the 1930s.

Later examples of Neutra's style are the 1960 Inadomi House (2238 Silver Lake Boulevard), with its airy feel, open floor plan, and reservoir views, and the 1957 Yew House (2226 Silver Lake Boulevard). The architectural offices that Neutra built in 1950 and occupied along with Dion, partner Richard Alexander, and other associates are

....

Richard Neutra's sketch of the Ohara house on Neutra Place.

at 2379 Glendale Boulevard, and currently in use by another firm, Built By Design.

Schindler, who like Neutra emigrated from Vienna, came to Los Angeles in the 1920s from Chicago, where he worked with and was greatly influenced by Frank Lloyd Wright. In Silver Lake, Schindler designed the spatially innovative, wood-and-concrete 1924 How House (2422 Silver Ridge Avenue), which features an interior made of L-shaped interlocking spaces around a diagonal axis and windows that come together in frameless glass corners. Its current owner, Lionel March, is a noted Schindler authority.

Silver Lake boasts many other notable Schindler structures, including the three-level, cantilevered Wilson House (2090 Redcliff Street), the Oliver House (2236 Micheltorena Street), the Droste House (2025 Kenilworth Avenue), the McAlmon House (2721 Waverly Drive), and the Falk Apartments at the northeast corner of Lucile and Carnation avenues.

An Asian design influence and connecting box shapes are featured in the 1939 Hawk House, at 2421 Silver Ridge Avenue, designed by Harwell Hamilton Harris, and in Ain's Scharlin House, set just below the crest of the hill at 2363 Silver Ridge Avenue. Scharlin House is a series of stucco boxes

Check it out: Silver Lake

Food and Drink

Cafe Tropical, 2900 Sunset Boulevard, (323) 661-8391. Cuban bakery and community hub. Doubles as regular meeting site for AA and NA.

Silverlake Lounge, 2906 Sunset Boulevard, (323) 666-2407. Bar, live music venue with weekend drag shows. Draws gays, straights, transvestites, and bohemian and working-class folk.

Alegria, 3510 Sunset Boulevard, (323) 913-1422. Bright, friendly neighborhood hang. Exceptional light, healthy Mexican food.

Millie's, 3524 Sunset Boulevard, (323) 664-0404. Personality-laden 25-seat counter serving breakfast, lunch for decades.

Madame Matisse, 3536 Sunset Boulevard, (323) 662-4862. A bistro meal at Denny's prices.

Cafe Stella, 3932 Sunset Boulevard, (323) 666-0265. Intimate, romantic bohemian bistro dedicated to classic French cuisine.

Netty's, 1700 Silver Lake Boulevard, (323) 662-8655. Fine food, ordered counter-style. Outside patio, brisk takeout business.

Back Door Bakery, 1710 Silver Lake Boulevard, (323) 662-7927. Muffins, croissants, baguettes, sandwiches, omelettes.

The Coffee Table, 2930 Rowena Avenue, (323) 644-8111. Java drinks, pastries, full meals. Spacious back patio. Popular with laptop novelists and screenwriters.

Specialty Shopping

The Snivling Sibbling, 3902 Sunset Boulevard, (323) 665-1616. Eclectic antiques and furnishings.

Edna Hart, 2941 Rowena Avenue, (323) 661-4070. Furniture, fabrics, decorative arts.

Casbah Cafe, 3900 Sunset Boulevard, (323) 664-7000. French-Moroccan mini-bazaar, with counter serving coffee, breakfast, lunch.

Special Events

Sunset Junction Street Fair, Sunset Boulevard between Edgecliffe Drive and Fountain Avenue, (323) 661-7771. Annual event in late August. Three stages with live music. Booths, carnival rides, food and drink, people-watching.

Silver Lake Film Festival, multiple venues (including the Vista Theatre), (323) 993-7225. Annual event celebrating the area's film heritage and creativity. Opening and closing night galas.

bound together by heavy wood trellises. Its large living room has a 10-foot ceiling, and its dining room, with balcony, affords panoramic views of the Griffith Park Observatory, Mt. Baldy, and downtown Los Angeles.

Community groups and architectural societies periodically offer tours of Silver Lake's Modernist homes. ⑤

East Hollywood

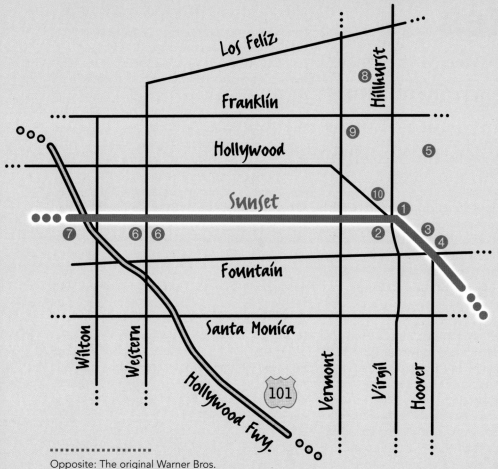

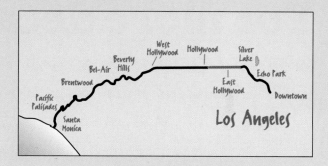

Los Angeles

1. **Vista Theatre/site of Griffith's *Intolerance* set**

2. **Site of Griffith-Fine Arts movie lot**

3. **KCET/site of Kalem and Monogram studios**

4. **Mack Sennett Stage/
site of Mabel Normand Studios**

5. **ABC Television Center Studios/
site of Vitagraph Studio**

6. **Sites of original Fox Studios lot**

7. **KTLA Channel 5/
site of original Warner Bros. movie lot**

8. **Los Feliz**

9. **Skylight Books**

10. **La Luz de Jesus Gallery/Wacko**

Opposite: The original Warner Bros.
studios on Sunset and Van Ness Avenue in 1927.

For more decades than it would

be kind to count, Gloria Swanson and her decaying mansion in *Sunset Boulevard* made the perfect metaphor for Hollywood—a former glamour-land turned irrelevant and tragic, forever plotting a comeback no one else was interested in.

But as the century turned, the plot twisted—and with recent new developments, it looks as if Hollywood may have found its happy ending, becoming once again a tourist mecca and occasional playground for the stars.

Little of the new cash and confidence has drifted into East Hollywood, however. For the most part, Sunset Boulevard between Fountain and Van Ness avenues is a dreary parade of storefronts selling nuts-and-bolts goods and tiny ethnic eateries, with one remarkable stretch devoted to hospitals and nontraditional religious centers.

The drab, workaday vibe makes it all the more remarkable that this corridor was once a virtual beehive of filmmaking activity. The trumpeting stone elephants that adorn the Babylon Court outside the new Academy Awards theater in the heart of Hollywood were copied from a D.W. Griffith movie set that stood for years near the corner of Sunset and Virgil Avenue. In their heyday, these blocks were the epicenter of the exciting new industry that would shape much of the history of Sunset Boulevard, not to mention that of the greater city of Los Angeles.

In 1908, the year Henry Ford introduced the affordable mass-production Model T automobile, Thomas Alva Edison patented the motion picture camera in the United States. Both inventions would have an incalculable effect on the growth of Los Angeles. Edison's invention was first put to use by U.S. moviemakers in New York, Chicago, and Philadelphia. But dependably mild and sunny weather—not to mention a strong desire to evade the process servers and thugs Edison's company hired to enforce his patent—lured filmmakers to California.

The inventor and the companies willing to pay him royalties had formed the Motion Picture Patent Co., also known in the day's parlance as "the Trust." Member companies, including Vitagraph, Selig, and Kalem, were among the first to operate studios on Sunset Boulevard. Non-Trust filmmakers were subject to lawsuits, smashed equipment, and a good bruising. It's no wonder the outlaw filmmakers liked Los Angeles; its proximity to the Mexican border meant they could disappear quickly should the need arise.

Between 1911 and 1913, the Los Angeles film industry exploded. Newcomers carrying satchels of money arrived in Los Angeles, usually at the train stations downtown. Upon taking the trip west along Sunset, they discovered the landscape opened up into a sleepy country town where vacant buildings, idle land, and farmers' fields could be cheaply had for studios. This was early Hollywood.

••••••••••••••••••••

Opposite: The interior of the Vista Theatre at Sunset and Hillhurst Avenue recalls the era when Egyptian decor was considered the height of exotica.

The first film company was established in 1911 at the corner of Sunset and Gower Street, and the first full-length feature was shot in 1913 near the corner of Sunset and Vine Street. Meanwhile, the blocks east of these locations were being commandeered by some of filmdom's most remarkable early figures.

D.W. Griffith established his headquarters where Sunset intersects Hollywood Boulevard. William Fox bought 20 acres at the corner of Sunset and Western Avenue and built a studio there. The Warner brothers established their empire in a mustard field at Sunset and Van Ness. Other film companies devoted to cranking out one- and two-reelers clustered nearby along Sunset, making it convenient for vendors, pitchmen, and aspiring actors to travel between them.

By 1912, about 3,000 people were employed as regulars or extras in movies in the Los Angeles area; 73 companies were at work, and more were arriving every month. Many of these companies made a picture or two and faded into oblivion, but others grew into major concerns.

Driving along Sunset today, it's almost impossible to visualize what this stretch of roadway must have been like when the street was frantic with picture-making activity. Just try to imagine riding the old Red Car trolley out Sunset from Union Station toward Hollywood one of those mornings. You might easily run into actors or extras dressed as Keystone Kops climbing aboard around Echo Park, or cowboy stuntmen from Mixville riding along in Silver Lake, or, wilder yet, Babylonian soldiers on their way to one of the world's most lavish movie sets. Yet they were all just people commuting to their day jobs.

The Vista Theatre, a thriving neighborhood movie house at the corner of Sunset and Hillhurst Avenue, is one of the few visible links to this nearly forgotten era. The striking Spanish Renaissance structure, built in 1923 as a playhouse by J.H. Woodhouse & Sons, offers moviegoers a trip back in time to the period of the 1920s when all things Egyptian were considered exotic and luxurious.

The Vista's box office is shaped like a shrine, modeled on the tomb of Queen Nefertari. The lobby features hand-painted hieroglyphics and the auditorium walls are lined with gilded Egyptian busts. The theater is also famous for its leg room, as half of its original 800 seats were removed for the comfort of patrons in a million-dollar

restoration in 1993 by the current owner, 5 Star Theaters. (Out front, the sidewalk features a "walk of fame" dedicated to such offbeat actors and filmmakers as Kenneth Anger; Martin Landau of *Ed Wood* fame; and Jon Favreau, whose *Swingers* captured the vibe of nearby Los Feliz.)

But it's the actual site of the Vista that is even more significant in movie lore. This is the spot where Griffith erected the monumental outdoor Babylon sets for his movie *Intolerance* in 1916. They stood at this corner three and a half years, drawing tourists from far and wide, and helped sear into the public mind the idea that Hollywood was a place where spectacular feats of the imagination could be willed into being.

David Wark Griffith was famous even before he came to Hollywood. For the Biograph company, based in New York, he had been cranking out audacious, groundbreaking one- and two-reel films for more than five years. While a flair for suspenseful melodrama made his work popular with audiences, it was such innovations as cross-cutting, close-ups, expressive lighting, and a moving cam-

....

D. W. Griffith is lifted in a hot air balloon while directing activities on the set of *Intolerance*. Opposite: The original set of Belshazzar's palace in *Intolerance*.

era that gained him the respect of his peers.

After a few visits to the West Coast, Griffith in 1913 moved his company west and took over the former Kinemascope studios at 4500 Sunset Boulevard, on the southwest corner of Sunset and Hillhurst just across the street from the present-day Vista. Dubbed Griffith–Fine Arts, the complex at various times went by the names Triangle and Mutual. But it was known in the business as simply "the Griffith lot."

Today, it's a lot of a far more prosaic kind— the parking lot of a Von's supermarket.

A former actor and poet— and reportedly not promising at either—the Kentucky-born film-maker was obsessed with an ambition to put poetry and grand ideas into the movies. At Biograph he'd crammed *The Call of the Wild* and *The Taming of the Shrew* into 15-minute one-reelers; now, as an independent, he set out to transform the movies. Soon he was making pictures seven and eight reels long.

In 1915, two years after he set up shop on Sunset, Griffith gambled everything on a three-hour Civil War epic called *The Birth of a Nation* (originally titled *The Clansman*) that became an enormous worldwide hit. The movie combined rank melodrama, historic sweep, astonishing sets, and realistic battle scenes along with Griffith's own majestic pictorial gift, and gave the world cinema such as it had never seen. Suddenly the movies were an art form, not just cheap entertainment for the masses. *The Birth of a Nation* was shown at the White House, where President Woodrow Wilson proclaimed it "like

history written with lightning."

Lamentably, *Birth*—based on a book by a hellfire Southern preacher—demonized blacks and glorified the Ku Klux Klan in the course of its simplistic melodrama. Out-raged African Americans and others protested at its Los Angeles premiere on February 8, 1915. Nonetheless, more than 100 million moviegoers around the world lined up to see it. Made for $110,000—an enormous sum at the time—the 12-reel picture took in nearly $60 million over the next nine years. Griffith became a huge celebrity, and money cascaded into his studio. Even before the invention of talking movies, a lot of wealthy people were suddenly excited about investing in the film business.

Although by now tremendously famous

and wealthy, Griffith felt unfairly stung by the accusations of racism and set out to redeem himself with an even more ambitious picture. This time he would weave four tales together to show how bigotry and injustice has been humanity's undoing through the ages. The theme was that salvation lay in love and charity. The image of a mother rocking a cradle was used to tie the stories together and, perplexingly, the project was titled *The Mother and the Law*. This name was emblazoned on a fence that ran along Sunset Boulevard, and so it was announced to all passers-by until finally the name of the project was changed to *Intolerance*, which was scarcely more appealing.

One of the four stories called for Griffith to re-create ancient Babylon, so that it could be overthrown by an army of Assyrians at the behest of a jealous priest.

The lot across the street from the Griffith studio had originally been leased to build Southern streets for *The Birth of a Nation*. Now, the great wall of Babylon went up along the northwest corner of the lot, designed by Walter "Spec" Hall and a team of Italian artisans. Eighty-foot attack tow-
•••••••••••••••••••••
D.W. Griffith directs a scene from *The Birth of a Nation*, his most famous work.

ers were built, and elephants were hired to push them into place. At one point, before filming could begin, Santa Ana winds nearly destroyed the towers, but they were held down with ropes and railroad ties. Finally, the huge battle scene was shot in which the king rides a chariot drawn by a team of horses along the top of the battle wall and a tower topples onto the attackers.

When that set was struck, a greater one was erected—the feast hall of Belshazzar, the king of Babylon. A great stairway, flanked with bulging pillars topped by trumpeting elephants, was built and richly carved and decorated. A two-level camera platform was devised in an elevator tower that rose more than 50 feet. This is the set that is frequently seen in pictures. Literally thousands of extras were outfitted for the battle scenes filmed on this set. During one period, when shooting took place along a body of water near San Pedro, thousands of men in the costumes of Babylonian soldiers would climb aboard Pacific Electric cars at Sunset and Hollywood and ride to the location each day.

The Babylon set drew tourists from all over. Everyone knew that D.W. Griffith was the Colossus of the picture world, and here was a fitting monument. Moreover, to moralists certain that Hollywood was the

Babylon of its time, here was the proof, out in the open for all to see and photograph.

A move in 1919 to preserve the Babylon set as a Hollywood monument got nowhere. It eventually crumbled and was demolished. Meanwhile, *Intolerance* baffled audiences upon release in 1916. Although critics today respect it as an important and pioneering work, the movie lost a great deal of money and was eventually regarded as a flop. The timing couldn't have helped—the film came out just as the United States was entering World War I, and few were in the mood for philosophical ruminations on the source of mankind's troubles.

Griffith survived, pragmatically returning to suspenseful melodramas to pay the bills. In 1919, he joined forces with Mary Pickford, Douglas Fairbanks, and Charlie Chaplin to create United Artists. Griffith made several more pictures considered important and successful, such as *Hearts of the World* (1918) and *Broken Blossoms* (1919), but his celebrity had peaked. In 1948, he died of a cerebral hemorrhage in the lobby of the Knickerbocker Hotel in Hollywood, where he'd been living. In 1962, crowds gathered once again at the old Griffith studios on Sunset, to watch them go up in flames as they were demolished.

Forty years later, the "Babylon Court" and archway beside the new Academy Awards theater at Hollywood and Highland Avenue pays homage to Griffith's boundary-pushing vision of what the movies could be. And in its re-creation of old Hollywood, Disney's California Adventure theme park in Anaheim features some of these same design elements.

Although Griffith was certainly among the most celebrated filmmakers of his day, there were plenty of others in the blocks around the Griffith lot. From 1912 onward, the building at Sunset and Hoover Street that now houses public television station KCET was used as a soundstage, first as home to the Kalem Co. and later as Monogram, which produced the *Dracula* films, various *Three Stooges* shorts, and a string of B pictures.

Comedienne Mabel Normand, after making her name tossing custard pies in Mack Sennett pictures, opened her own production studio near the corner of Sunset and Fountain. Today, this triangle-shaped building is a rental facility known as the Mack Sennett Stage. A few blocks away, at the corner of Prospect Avenue and Talmadge Street—named for Norma Talmadge, the silent film star—was the busy

Vitagraph studio, part of Edison's Trust. Vitagraph was eventually absorbed by Warner Bros., and later became the ABC Television studios, as it remains today.

On the stretch of Sunset closer to central Hollywood, a soon-to-be major player had come to town to make his mark on the movies. In 1916, impresario William Fox purchased 20 acres at the southeast and southwest corners of Sunset and Western and established Fox Studios. A hard-driving Hungarian immigrant, Fox had already made a fortune in theater operations in New York. He soon had leading lady Theda Bara, director John Ford, writer H.G. Wells, and producers David Belasco and Howard Hawks (later better known as a director) on his payroll, all part of a team that Fox promised would

. . . .

Above: The early William Fox studios at Sunset and Western Avenue. Right: Scientific Films was one of the scores of studios that came and went in the early days of Hollywood filmmaking. Opposite: The set of the film *Noah's Ark*, released in 1929 by Warner Bros. The spot today is occupied by the studios of ABC Television.

create "the finest in movie entertainment."

Keenly interested in the possibility of adding sound to the movie experience, the showman invested heavily in a sound system called Movietone. He came close to winning the race to create "talkies" when he captured the sounds of Charles Lindbergh's airplane taking off in an attempt to reach Paris. Fox had the historic takeoff played in theaters, preceded by much ballyhoo.

In 1935, Fox merged his operation with

Joseph Schenck and Darryl F. Zanuck's Twentieth Century Pictures, and Twentieth Century-Fox was created. The bulk of filmmaking was shifted to the present-day lot near what is now Century City, but Fox continued to use the Sunset lot until the 1960s. Where people now shop for discount groceries at the corner of Sunset and Western, dreams were once spun onto celluloid. That's why they call it "Lost Angeles."

By 1919, Fox had a competitive new neighbor a few blocks west on Sunset. The Warner brothers—Albert, Harry, Sam, and Jack—built a soundstage in a former mustard field near the corner of Sunset and Van Ness. As soon as they could afford it, they built bigger and grander facilities—including the elaborate Greek-columned executive building. Even today, the classical Eastern-looking building appears pretentious and out of place on this stretch of Sunset. But the Warners were from back East and the building was their way of announcing to their bigger and better-funded competitors that they were here to stay. It proved to be an accurate boast.

The new Warner Bros. studios made a series of comedies in the Mack Sennett mold, then set out to distinguish itself by focusing on works of social relevance and literary qual-

ity. Adaptations of F. Scott Fitzgerald's *The Beautiful and the Damned* (1922) and Sinclair Lewis' *Main Street* (1923) followed, among many other ambitious projects.

Actor John Barrymore became Warner's big prestige star, but in reality most of the studio's bills were being paid by a dog, Rin-Tin-Tin, who had shot to fame performing heroic deeds in a series of movies. "Rinty," as he was known to his legion of young fans, was a German Shepherd abandoned in France by retreating German soldiers. The canine had an extraordinary ability to take direction and perform tricks. But contrary to the image manufactured by Warners' public relations team, the dog had a nasty temper and was loathed by the many crew members whom he had attacked or bitten. To keep the dog happy, the studio hired an orchestra to play for him on location and fed him Chateaubriand steaks. Between Rinty and Barrymore, who was often drunk and temperamental on the set, the Warner brothers were getting an early education in the star system.

By far the most important thing that happened during the Warner brothers' tenure on Sunset Boulevard was the breakthrough they achieved in motion picture sound.

Sound had been a dream of filmmakers

from the beginning. Ingenious minds from Edison to Griffith, Fox, and Disney had tackled the daunting task of finding a way to synchronize sound with moving images. The process was hugely problematic. But with Fox, their neighbor on Sunset, gaining on them, the Warner brothers persevered and in 1927 achieved a definitive breakthrough with *The Jazz Singer*, much of which was shot on the Sunset lot.

The Jazz Singer premiered October 7, 1927, at the Warner theater in New York, playing to a top-flight society audience. By all accounts, you had to be there. Al Jolson, in the title role as an aspiring young singer, performed on film with electric excitement, fully aware he was ushering in a revolution. When he burst into song with "Dirty Hands, Dirty Face," the audience went wild. He then ad-libbed the prophetic lines that were the first ever spoken in an American movie: "Wait a minute, wait a minute! You ain't heard nothing yet!"

In a state of hysterical excitement, Jolson then sang "Tootsie" with everything he had. The songs kept coming, as did an excited speech the Jolson character delivered to his mother about all the gifts he could buy her when he was rich. The audience cheered and cheered and refused to

sit down. It was a complete and utter triumph. Eyewitnesses remember shivering in the certainty that the world would never be the same.

Ironically, the Warner brothers were not there to share the applause. Sam Warner was on his deathbed in Los Angeles after a series of operations gone bad. On hearing the news, the other brothers—Harry, Albert, and Jack—hastily departed New York the day before the premiere to be by his side. Unable to charter a plane in those early days of air travel, they took the train to the coast and, sadly, arrived too late to say their goodbyes.

The movie industry was irrevocably changed by the advent of sound. Warner Bros. made its first all-talking movie, *The Lights of New York*, the following year. The work was an immediate success and, all over town, it was suddenly talkies or nothing. The development was a calamity for some silent film stars, many of whom were neither trained nor gifted in elocution. Some had shrill voices, some had heavy accents; others were not capable of remembering their lines. But for every Mae Marsh who went by the wayside, there was a Barbara Stanwyck or Bette Davis stepping up to snap off dialogue with sizzle and aplomb, and the machinery rolled on.

In late 1930, Warner Bros. moved its headquarters to the Burbank real estate of First National Studios, which became the lot it occupies today. The Sunset stages remained in use for filming and other operations for many years. Western star Gene Autry and his Golden West Broadcasting Company later moved into the Greek-columned executive building. In recent years, the building has housed the KTLA Channel 5 news operation. As an affiliate of the Warner-owned WB network, the station remains within the extended family of the lot's original tinseltown family, even continuing to use some of the pioneering, barn-like soundstages.

Healing Powers

Immense centers devoted to physical healing and spiritual growth or reorientation dominate several blocks of Sunset between Vermont and Normandie avenues in East Hollywood.

Kaiser Permanente hospital is part of a health-care network named for industrialist Henry J. Kaiser and an early business venture of his located near Permanente Creek in the San Francisco Bay Area. The Oakland-based health maintenance organization evolved from prepaid health-care programs developed in the 1930s and 1940s by Kaiser and surgeon Sidney R. Garfield to cover thousands of workers on the Colorado Aqueduct (one of the three main pipelines bringing water into Los Angeles) and the Grand Coulee Dam.

The successful experiment—in which workers enrolled voluntarily and paid five cents a day for insurance covering job-related injuries—might have ended there, but history intervened. With the outbreak of World War II, Kaiser-managed shipyards and steel foundries, including a major shipbuilding operation in the Bay Area, landed massive contracts that called for employing tens of thousands of workers, and the med-

ical plan was expanded to cover them. In 1945, after the war ended and the shipyards closed, the plan was opened to the public. Enrollment surpassed 300,000 within the first 10 years, largely because of the support of two unions: the International Longshoremen and Warehousemen Union and the Retail Clerks Union, which helped bring the health plan to Los Angeles. Now the nation's largest HMO, Kaiser serves 8.1 million members in nine states. The Kaiser hospital on Sunset Boulevard has operated there since 1953.

Childrens Hospital across the street opened in 1914 but its roots date to the turn of the 20th century, when a remarkable group of women determined that medical care should be available to all children of the city, regardless of a family's ability to pay. In 1900 the women organized a public meeting to propose the creation of a hospital dedicated to that cause, as no such facility existed south of San Francisco. (Los Angeles County Hospital had no children's ward until 1912.) Dr. LeMoyne Wills, who attended the meeting, helped advance the idea to civic leaders and other potential contributors. The hospital was launched and formally incorporated in 1901 with a board of directors composed entirely of women, who tackled fund-raising and ran the business affairs.

Among the early directors were Kate Page Crutcher, long-time president of the Childrens Hospital Society and a key force in providing direction and motivation for the hospital from 1907 to 1947, and Emma Phillips, another founding member of the Childrens Hospital Society

who bequeathed the Sunset Boulevard property to the hospital.

The first site was a small house downtown at Alpine and Castelar (now Hill) streets, in the vicinity of today's Chinatown. Doctors, some of them the husbands of the founders, worked on a volunteer basis, a practice that continued for decades. The little hospital grew quickly, as leading families made sizable donations. The women accelerated their fund-raising, and the new facility on Sunset opened in February 1914. In 1926, its silver anniversary year, the hospital admitted 9,000 children and treated 40,000 as outpatients.

. . . .

Opposite: In 1900 Dr. LeMoyne Wills was an early supporter of efforts to create Childrens Hospital, shown above nearly a century later.

Today, Childrens Hospital treats more than 250,000 patients annually and has a renowned research institute and specialties in such advanced procedures as the treatment of pediatric heart disease, AIDS, cancer, and organ transplants from living donors. With a staff of more than 2,800 and an enormous cadre of committee volunteers, it continues to shine as an outstanding example of the philanthropic tradition in Los Angeles.

Another leading hospital, Cedars of Lebanon, stood next door to Childrens Hospital for decades, beginning in the 1920s. But in 1976, that property fronting at 4810 Sunset Boulevard was taken over by the Church of Scientology, which has since amassed sizable real estate holdings throughout Hollywood. The modern Scientology building facing Sunset contains a bookstore and reception area where visitors are welcome, as recruitment is always a priority.

Founded in the early 1950s by writer L. Ron Hubbard and his followers, Scientology at its core is a series of courses based on Hubbard's published works. The aim is unburdening parishioners of spiritually traumatizing past experiences. As the courses progress, at ever-higher tuition levels, they describe the interplanetary warfare conducted by the "thetans," or immortal souls, who supposedly created the universe and everything in it.

Even if Hubbard's theories sound like science fiction to many, they are the basis of a worldwide movement that claims 6.5 million adherents. Some of these members can be seen walking around the Sunset campus in distinctive naval uniforms. Although the philosophy rejects notions of God and heaven, Scientology is recognized as a religion by the federal government. In 1993, the church and its more than 150 associated corporate entities were granted tax-exempt status after decades of bitter feuding with the IRS. The church has since begun a drive to extend its reach into schools and businesses by way of literacy and consulting programs.

A block of Berendo Street adjacent to the property was renamed L. Ron Hubbard Way in 1996, 10 years after Hubbard died of a stroke on his California ranch near San Luis Obispo. The older blue buildings to the rear of the property contain living quarters and classrooms for Scientology members, and are of some architectural interest, as

they contain elements of the 1920s Zigzag Moderne and 1930s Streamline Moderne Art Deco styles.

The Scientology campus' western neighbor on Sunset is the home of another religious movement, the Self-Realization Fellowship, founded by Paramahansa Yogananda, a swami from India. A universal "church of all religions" that has its Los Angeles headquarters in Mount Washington, it opened on this site in 1942. The church has yet another site on Sunset, at the western end in Pacific Palisades. The fellowship is dedicated to communion with a universal God and a spirit of Oneness linking all religions and races. The chapel was transported from another site and extensively remodeled by the monks and nuns. The grounds include a bookstore; a large auditorium; living quarters for resident monastics; meditation gardens; and space for lectures, services, classes, and yoga.

Los Feliz

At the junction of Sunset and Hillhurst Avenue, where Silver Lake blends into East Hollywood near the historic Vista Theatre, the increasingly vibrant and popular neighborhood of Los Feliz unfolds several blocks to the north.

Equal parts old money and bohemian flair, Los Feliz, like much of the eastern side of Los Angeles, is blooming from an infusion of cash, optimism, and creative energy that took hold during the prosperity of the mid-1990s.

On the gentle slopes north of wide, tree-lined Los Feliz Boulevard lie the elegant mansions built in the 1920s for doctors, bankers, and showbiz folk—most of which have changed hands only once or twice since then. Some are European or Italianate architectural gems; dozens more were designed by such Modernist masters as Frank Lloyd Wright, Richard Neutra, Rudolph Schindler, Gregory Ain, and John Lautner.

South of the boulevard, centered

....
Left: The Self-Realization Fellowship Temple in Hollywood is one of three facilities the church operates in Los Angeles. Right: A couple swings at the Derby Club in Los Feliz.

around Hillhurst and Vermont avenues, is a bohemian mecca of restaurants, jazz joints, bookstores, cafes, and art-house theaters that competes with Silver Lake as the hipster habitat of choice.

Here is where ardent fans of swing band music dance at the Derby Club, both in real life and the movie *Swingers*; here is where hepcats gather at the lost-in-time Dresden Room to hear lounge music.

On Vermont, in particular, are rows of sidewalk cafes and eclectic shops with an emphasis on retro and vintage clothing and furniture, as well as reading matter and videos for those with adventurous tastes. ◉

Check it out: East Hollywood and Los Feliz

East Hollywood

Espresso Mi Cultura, 5625 Hollywood Boulevard (just west of Western Avenue), (323) 461-0808. Book and coffee shop with focus on Latino arts, frequented by Gen-Mexers, sidewalk intellectuals.

Thailand Plaza, 5321 Hollywood Boulevard (2nd floor), (323) 993-9000. Courtyard-style eatery featuring array of restaurants and entertainment by Thai Elvis impersonator, plus a Thai grocery and bookstore. Surrounding blocks feature dozens of Thai restaurants, many open well past midnight; all part of the Thai Town area officially designated in 1998.

Tiki Ti, 4427 Sunset Boulevard (between Hollywood Boulevard and Fountain Avenue), (323) 669-9381. Tropical drinks, Polynesian decor in tiny, rowdy watering hole.

El Cid, 4212 Sunset Boulevard, (323) 668-0318. Live flamenco since 1961, in courtyard replica of 16th-century Spanish tavern, also cocktails, sangria, tapas, paella.

Zankou Chicken, 5065 Sunset Boulevard (at Normandie Avenue), (323) 665-7842. Rotisserie chicken hole-in-the-wall famed for killer garlic sauce, hummus, shawerma.

Hollywood Billiards, 5750 Hollywood Boulevard, (323) 465-0115. Spacious billiards hall with open tournaments, karaoke, live entertainment. Adjacent restaurant with elegant fountain courtyard, northern Italian cuisine.

Paru's Indian Vegetarian Restaurant, 5140 Sunset Boulevard, (323) 661-7600. Friendly South Indian neighborhood eatery. Tree-filled outdoor patio.

La Luz de Jesus Gallery/Wacko, 4633 Hollywood Boulevard, (323) 666-7667. Art gallery combined with vast emporium of books, gifts, and pop cultural flotsam and jetsam.

Sunset Boulevard Nursery, 4368 Sunset Boulevard, (323) 661-1642. Deep, excellent section of plants, seedlings, herbs, bulbs, gardening supplies.

Special Events

Eastside Art Crawl. Annual weekend open house at galleries and studios in Los Feliz, Silver Lake, and East Hollywood. Held in late September (check arts listings in newspaper).

Los Feliz Village Street Festival. Music, booths, and crafts are featured at the annual hobnob held alternately on Hillhurst and Vermont avenues on a late October weekend every year (check arts listings or www.la.com).

Los Feliz

Skylight Books, 1818 North Vermont Avenue, (323) 660-1175. Literary hub, frequent signings by noted authors, extensive section on Los Angeles and local subjects.

The Derby Club, 4500 Los Feliz Boulevard, (323) 663-8979. Cocktails, bands, retro swing dancing in hat-shaped landmark.

The Dresden Room, 1760 North Vermont Avenue, (323) 665-4294. Restaurant and kitschy bar featuring lost-in-the-1970s lounge act Marty and Elayne.

Figaro Cafe, 1804 North Vermont Avenue, (323) 662-2874. Time travel to 1930s Paris in this incredibly authentic recreation of a Left Bank brasserie, with an adjacent bakery and sidewalk tables. French cuisine, Gallic wine list.

Mexico City, 2121 Hillhurst Avenue, (323) 661-7227. Authentic, upscale Mexican cuisine and margaritas in comfortable room with booths, bar, avenue view.

Good Luck Bar, 1514 Hillhurst Avenue, (323) 666-3524. Ornate, beautiful Chinese-themed bar featuring exotic cocktails and comfy lounge. Vista Theatre-adjacent.

Squaresville, 1800 North Vermont Avenue, (323) 669-8464. Weird, wild, and vintage clothing and accessories.

Pre-movie "curtain show" at vintage El Capitan
Theatre on Hollywood Boulevard.

Central Hollywood

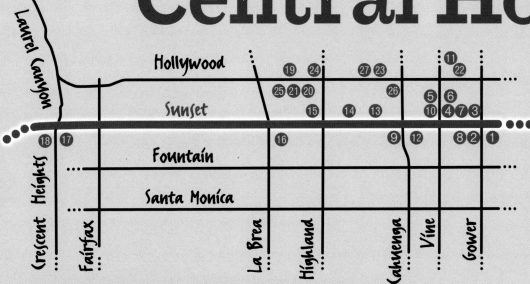

1. **Sunset-Gower studios/site of original Columbia Pictures studio**

2. **Gower Gulch/site of Poverty Row movie companies**

3. **CBS broadcast studios/site of first Hollywood filmmaking company in 1911**

4. **Washington Mutual Bank/site of NBC Radio City studios/site of Cecil B. DeMille's "The Squaw Man"**

5. **James A. Doolittle Theatre/ site of Lux Radio Theater**

6. **Site of Brown Derby restaurant**

7. **The Palladium**

8. **Nickelodeon soundstage/ site of Earl Carroll Theater**

9. **Site of Hollywood Canteen (1940s)**

10. **Site of Wallichs Music City**

11. **Capitol Records**

12. **Cinerama Dome**

13. **Hollywood Athletic Club**

14. **The Crossroads of the World**

15. **Hollywood High School**

16. **Site of Charlie Chaplin studios and home**

17. **Site of Schwab's Drugstore**

18. **Site of Garden of Allah apartments**

19. **Grauman's Chinese Theatre**

20. **Egyptian Theatre/American Cinematheque**

21. **El Capitan Theatre**

22. **Pantages Theatre**

23. **Warner Pacific Theatre**

24. **Kodak Theatre/site of Hollywood Hotel, built in 1903**

25. **Hollywood Roosevelt Hotel/site of first Academy Awards in 1929**

26. **Raymond Chandler Square**

The crash of the wrecking ball, the chisel of the drill, the clank of steel girders being lifted into place. These were the sounds defining central Hollywood at the turn of the millennium. Fueled by the cash and confidence of the 1990s economic boom, revitalization of the Hollywood

core—a dream held fast for decades by die-hard believers—was finally being realized.

After years of neglect, Hollywood is again getting its turn in the limelight, a chance to showcase the magic and fantasy on which it was built by becoming the permanent home of the Oscars ceremony and a host of new attractions.

Still, a visit to Hollywood today is greatly enhanced by an understanding of its history—both the early years of filmmaking and the glamorous era of the 1930s and 1940s when nearby film and radio studios, night-clubs and upscale shops made the sidewalks a parade of star-gazing and excitement.

. . . .

Opposite: Subtle reminders of one's whereabouts can be spotted once Sunset Boulevard crosses into Hollywood.

Perhaps the best place to start a tour of the Hollywood stretch of Sunset Boulevard is where it intersects with Gower Street. From here, you see sound-stages, post-production houses, a swank restaurant catering to the entertainment industry, and directly up Gower on the hillside—just in case you missed the vibe—the 50-foot white letters spelling it all out: HOLLYWOOD.

The huge Sunset-Gower studios, now a rental facility for shooting television shows, movies, and commercials, was the original home of Columbia Pictures in the 1920s. The stylish Pinot restaurant adjacent was formerly an upscale eatery called the Columbia Bar and Grill, and the locale has always been a favorite for film colony dining and deal-making.

Across the street, the Old West-style shopping and eating area known as Gower Gulch was colonized by small, independent movie companies in the early years of film-making. The corner's western theme and nickname were inspired by the cowboy extras who hung

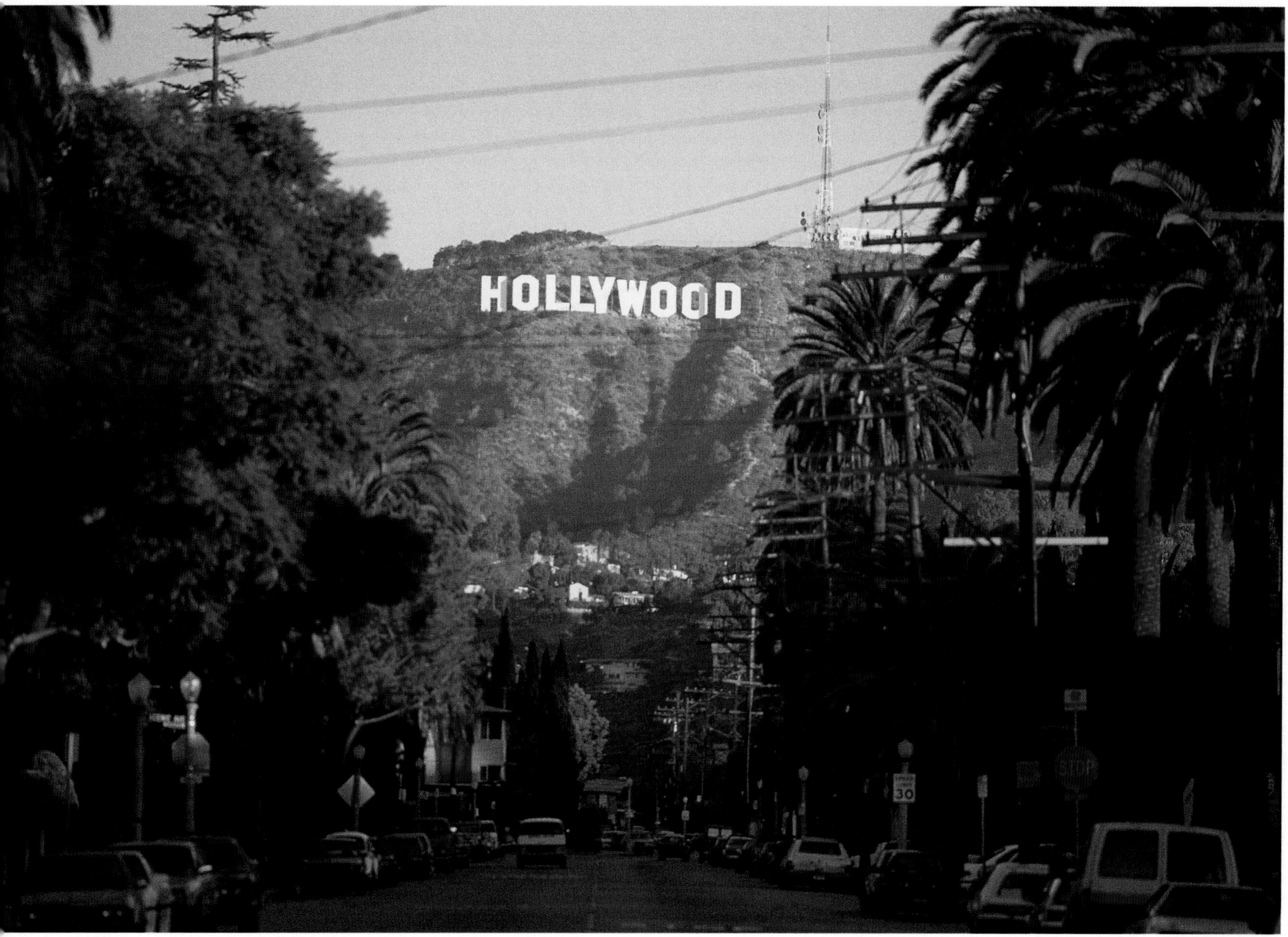
HOLLYWOOD
30

around waiting for parts at the early studios.

The northwest corner, where the CBS radio and television news complex stands, was the site chosen in 1911 by the first film company to operate in Hollywood. After CBS moved in, it became a hot spot for stars and star-gazing during the golden radio era of the 1930s.

Directly south on Gower are the blocks-long stages of Paramount Studios, the last of the original major studios to have a Hollywood presence. Home of the opulent, classic gates seen in the movie *Sunset Boulevard*—they front on Melrose Avenue— this facility offers studio tours and attracts long lines of people waiting to form the audiences for live television tapings.

Before the movie-makers came to town, things were much different. Hollywood was merely a quiet, rural, God-fearing Protestant community. But when the locals passed blue laws outlawing the sale of alcohol, they idled an establishment called the Blondeau Tavern at the corner of Sunset and Gower. This led the proprietor to seek new income, and in October of 1911 he rented the building to a filmmaker, David Horsley, ironically paving the way for the scourge that was Hollywood.

Horsley made the former tavern the West Coast headquarters of his New Jer-

sey-based Nestor Films. The company— the first to set up shop in Hollywood— immediately began churning out two-reel silent movies, most of them Westerns shot outdoors on a wooden platform rigged with muslin to diffuse the strong California sunlight. Mild winter weather allowed the company to crank out a steady stream of pictures, a fact that didn't escape the notice of Horsley's competitors back

home. Within months, he was joined by 15 film companies operating nearby.

In May 1912, Nestor Films was acquired by movie pioneer Carl Laemmle, who merged it with his Universal Film Manufacturing Co. to create the basis for modern film giant Universal Studios. In 1915, the company moved from Sunset and Gower to ranch land just over the Cahuenga Pass in the San Fernando Valley, where Universal Studios remains today.

In 1913, a movie-making team from the East composed of Cecil B. DeMille, Jesse Lasky, Samuel Goldfish (later Goldwyn), and Arthur Friend arrived in Hollywood. The ambitious young men rented a barn located a short way north of the corner of Sunset and

··········

Above: Nestor Films at Sunset and Gower in 1913. Right: Sunset and Vine in 1925, when Famous Players-Lasky studios was at its peak. Opposite: Little girls pose in the barren intersection of Sunset and Gower, 1905.

Vine Street, and from there made *The Squaw Man* (1914), a western based on a successful Broadway play that became the first full-length feature film shot in Hollywood.

DeMille ran the company from his office in the barn, while the barn owner, Jacob Stern, continued to use the other half of the rustic building to shelter his horses. When the animals were watered, the water ran into DeMille's office, and he was forced to either wear galoshes or put his feet in a wastebasket. The barn, as well as DeMille's office and its original furnishings, have been preserved as the home of the Hollywood Heritage Museum and moved to 2100 Highland Avenue, across from the Hollywood Bowl. (Today the former site of the barn is a parking lot adjacent to a branch of the Washington Mutual Bank. Within the bank is a mural, nearly hidden on the front wall, commemorating

the historic events at this location.)

The Lasky company grew to occupy two full blocks and in 1916 merged with Adolph Zukor's outfit to form Famous Players–Lasky Corp. Zukor brought in a talented young Canadian actress, Gladys Smith, who took the name Mary Pickford and became the screen's first female superstar. In 1926, the company moved south from Sunset to the corner of Gower and Melrose Avenue and was eventually renamed Paramount Pictures.

By 1920, the movies were attracting an audience of 35 million people weekly, each willing to plunk down five cents to be transported into a flickering world of romance, thrills, and excitement. There was a fortune to be made filling the seemingly endless demand for new programs, and a great many independent producers, with scarcely enough capital to finance a single two-reeler, stepped up to give it a try.

The southwest corner of Sunset and Gower became a magnet for these fly-by-nighters, and the low-budget enclave became known as Poverty Row to movie insiders. To the public, however, it was Gower Gulch—named for the would-be cowboy actors—and so it remains today.

Typically, Poverty Row operators rented facilities long enough to make their movies, then disappeared. But some took hold. Companies like Republic, Mascot, Monogram, and Grand National persisted on the corner for decades, making movies they sold to independent small-town theaters, until television came along in the 1950s and destroyed their market.

Columbia Pictures had ignominious beginnings on the corner, but grew into the major studio that today is Japanese-financed Sony Pictures Entertainment, based in Culver City. In the early 1920s, mogul-to-be Harry Cohn came out from New York to establish the picture-making operation of the Columbia Broadcasting Company. With far more ambition than capital, he was forced to start by renting facilities at Poverty Row. His amused competitors referred to his modest CBC operation as "Corned Beef and Cabbage," which rankled him to no end. So he changed the name to Columbia Pictures and borrowed financing to lease long-term facilities on the southeast corner of Sunset and Gower, launching the new studio on January 10, 1924.

In 1928, the tight-fisted Cohn agreed to pay Frank Capra, a director of slapstick comedies for Mack Sennett, $1,000 to helm a movie for him. Cohn quickly recognized Capra's talent, and hired him for picture after picture. At the height of the Depression, Capra and screenwriter Robert Riskin fashioned a screwball romantic comedy with the message that the poor have more fun. The movie starred Clark Gable as a reporter and Claudette Colbert as a runaway heiress. *It Happened One Night* went on to win Best Picture of 1934 and sweep the Academy Awards, and Columbia was catapulted to the top of the heap.

By the 1940s, Columbia was entrenched as a major Hollywood studio and introduced a string of stars: Jimmy Stewart and Jean Arthur in *Mr. Smith Goes to Washington* and red-headed Rita Hayworth in *Gilda* and *The Lady From Shanghai* in the 1940s; Marlon Brando in *On the Waterfront* in the 1950s; and Barbra Streisand in *Funny Girl* in the 1960s.

Columbia became the last of the majors to leave Sunset Boulevard when, between 1970 and 1972, the studio moved out of what had become a 14-acre complex stretching between Gower and Beachwood Drive. Initially, Columbia settled into a complex in Burbank, but later moved to the former MGM lot in Culver City, where it remains today as Sony Pictures Entertainment.

Movies weren't the only entertainment

NBC Radio City, Sunset and Vine, Hollywood, California

After work, the stars gravitated to nearby hangouts on Vine like the Brown Derby and Clara Bow's It Room at the Hollywood Plaza Hotel. Vine Street was tremendously glamorous in the 1930s, attracting stylish folk at all hours of the day and night. The Lux Radio Theater operated at 615 Vine Street, where Cecil B. DeMille hosted a weekly national broadcast featuring top stars performing live radio versions of popular movies. Episodes of *Your Hit Parade* were also broadcast from the site. In 1954, the facility became the Huntington Hartford, an important live theater venue, and later, the James A. Doolittle Theatre, producing Tony- and Pulitzer Prize–winning plays.

The Hollywood nightclubs of the 1930s and 1940s capitalized on the fever of the big band era in the pre-television years. The Palladium (6215 Sunset Boulevard, at Argyle Avenue) opened in 1940, constructed for $1.6 million by Norman Chandler, then publisher of the *Los Angeles Times*. Designed for maximum razzle-dazzle, with a kidney-shaped dance floor large enough for 7,500 patrons, it was dubbed the "Super Ballroom" by the press and was the ulti-

born along this section of Sunset. Beginning in the late 1930s—the "Golden Age of Radio"—Sunset Boulevard became the radio capital of the West Coast, housing NBC and CBS, alongside several local stations. ABC joined the lineup in 1951.

The swanky Art Deco edifice of NBC Radio City dominated Sunset and Vine from 1938 to 1964, occupying the northeast corner where the Washington Mutual Bank now stands. The huge complex included eight studios for live broadcasts. Fans gath-

ered every night at the parking lot on Vine, hoping to glimpse such stars as Bob Hope, Bing Crosby, Dinah Shore, Fred Allen, Frank Sinatra, and Perry Como.

CBS built the facility that still stands at Sunset and Gower and houses the local KCBS television news, KNX radio, and other operations. Before the growth of television, all CBS radio programs were broadcast from here, including the popular *Art Linkletter's House Party*.

Celebrity Central

The venerable Brown Derby restaurant at 1628 Vine Street was perhaps the most famous and enduring of Hollywood's celebrity magnets. It wasn't shaped like a hat—that was the original Derby restaurant on Wilshire Boulevard—but was done in an elegant Spanish Moroccan style. The architect, Carl Jules Weyl, also designed Rick's Cafe for the movie *Casablanca* (1942).

The Cobb salad was introduced here by owner Bob Cobb, a bon vivant much loved by his famous clientele. Cobb also owned a baseball team, the Hollywood All-Stars.

The Brown Derby drew stars, press, and publicity like no place else in the 1930s and 1940s. Marlene Dietrich once startled diners by entering in men's clothing. A pair of male comics, Wheeler and Woolsey, got up and dashed into a nearby department store, returning dressed in drag to an appreciative audience. The restaurant persevered until it was razed in the early 1980s. Today it's—you guessed it—a parking lot.

THE BROWN DERBY RESTAURANT — 1628 N. VINE ST. — HOLLYWOOD, CALIF.

mate gig for the swing bands of the day. Tommy Dorsey was the opening night attraction and Glenn Miller soon followed. Beginning in 1961, Lawrence Welk led his orchestra at the Palladium every other Saturday for 15 years. His television show, complete with bubble machine, was broadcast from the site. Today, the venue presents rock concerts and other live shows.

The renowned Earl Carroll Theater was across the street at 6230 Sunset, on the site of a soundstage that is now used to tape shows for the Nickelodeon cable channel. A showman in the Ziegfeld tradition, Carroll made a big splash on the night-life scene when he opened in December 1938, pre-

. . . .

The Palladium during a brief closure, in 1993. Opposite, left: Betty Hutton and aspiring starlets entertain troops at the Hollywood Canteen, in 1945. Opposite, center: A menu cover from the Moulin Rouge supper club, which later occupied the Earl Carroll site. Opposite, right: Gorgeous Earl Carroll showgirls, appearing in the 1930s movie *Murder At the Vanities*.

senting 60 nearly nude showgirls on two revolving stages. The neon sign he hung above the door—which today can be seen over the pedestrian mall at Universal City-Walk—declared: "Through these doors pass the most beautiful girls in the world."

Carroll's showroom was extravagantly tacky, with patent leather ceilings and 6,200 feet of neon lighting. A wall of fame outside featured the handprints and signatures of the many stars the place attracted. Carroll died in a plane crash in 1948, along with his lead showgirl, Beryl Wallace. In the 1960s, the venue became the Aquarius Theater, housing a live production of *Hair*. Later, it was the home of the "Star Search" TV show.

The spot where a parking garage now stands on the southwest corner of Sunset and Cahuenga boulevards is another significant site in the annals of Hollywood night life. During World War II, this corner was home to the Hollywood Canteen, where military personnel flocked to mingle and dance with the stars, who volunteered to entertain them.

For nearly 40 years beginning in 1942, a store called Wallichs Music City occupied the corner of Sunset and Vine, selling records, radios, and musical instruments. Owner Glenn Wallichs joined Buddy DeSylva and musician Johnny Mercer to form the storefront operation that became Capitol Records. By 1956 they were able to finance the distinctive tower headquarters that stands further up Vine. The label went on to distribute the music of Sinatra, the Beach

Boys, and the Beatles. The 13-story circular tower at 1750 Vine Street, which resembles a stack of 45s on a record spindle, became a Hollywood landmark, topped each Christmas by a sparkling tree. Sinatra recorded with an orchestra in the first-floor studios; an outside mural commemorates some of the label's other artists, including Nat King Cole. Today a new retail and apartment complex is planned for the corner of Sunset and Vine.

The animation company Klasky-Csupo, which helped develop and originate "The Simpsons" and also produces the "Rugrats" television show and movies, moved its headquarters to a former car dealership at 6353 Sunset Boulevard. An adjacent store sells animation-inspired toys, videos, and souvenirs.

Film students from many countries attend the Los Angeles Film School, next door at 6363 Sunset. The institution was launched in 1999 to provide a certified, practical education for would-be filmmakers. It frequently hosts public screenings and well-known guest lecturers from the movie industry.

....

The landmark Capitol Records building and its lobby, which boasts more than 100 gold records. Opposite: The Cinerama Dome theater under construction in 1963, the year it opened, and a completed view, in 1992.

A major new retail complex and a movie multiplex are being developed around the Cinerama Dome, the unusual golf-ball-shaped theater at 6360 Sunset. Nearly bulldozed by developers in the late 1990s, the shrine to a now-defunct movie process was saved by preservationists, who recognized its unique contribution to the Hollywood dreamscape. Designed by architect Welton Becket, the Dome opened in 1963 to accommodate the premiere of the Cinerama feature *It's a Mad Mad Mad Mad World*, a comedy caper starring Spencer Tracy and Milton Berle. The wide-screen, three-projector Cinerama system proved to be a flash in the pan, nearly obsolete by the time the theater opened. But the Dome,

with its huge, curved screen and spacious 937-seat auditorium, became a favorite venue of film buffs, who flock there for 70mm screenings, restored reissues, and splashy premieres.

Farther down the boulevard at 6525 Sunset (at Hudson Avenue) is the Hollywood Athletic Club, a former playhouse for the stars that is now used for movie shoots and private events. After opening on New Year's Eve in 1923 as a top-drawer gymnasium loaded with extras, including a 25-yard swimming pool, guest rooms, billiards, and a barber shop, the facility served as the area's original "boys club" for much of the 1920s and 1930s.

For years, the club doubled as an elegant crash pad and retreat for members like John Barrymore, Errol Flynn, W.C. Fields, John Wayne, Charlie Chaplin, Clark Gable, Rudolph Valentino, and Anthony Quinn. Their bad-boy antics became legendary. Fields once wrapped a mistress in a rug to smuggle her upstairs. Wayne supposedly bounced billiard balls off passing cars from a balcony. In 1942, members drinking at the bar hatched a scheme to prolong their fun with a newly deceased pal, actor John Barrymore. They stole his body from the McKinley mortuary, located on Sunset at Horn Avenue, and propped it up in a chair at Flynn's house, then waited drunkenly to observe Flynn's reaction when he returned home. Reportedly, it gave the swashbuckler quite a fright.

Esther Williams was the only woman allowed to swim at the pool, where movie "Tarzans" Johnny Weismuller and Buster Crabbe worked as lifeguards. Not just stars used the club. By 1926, it had 1,000 members and sponsored teams in a dozen sports. The facility later went through various incarnations, becoming a Jewish seminary in 1958 and a Russian nightclub in the 1980s.

In 1990, the Athletic Club reopened as an upscale billiards palace and retro night-

The Crossroads of the World, 1938, when it was still an excitingly modern shopping center. Opposite: The Hollywood Athletic Club, circa 1928, and the design from an early club matchbook cover.

club and flourished through most of the decade, once again drawing stars—this time the likes of Sean Penn, Mickey Rourke, and Cameron Diaz, among others. The nightclub closed in 2000, but the space is often rented for private events and filming.

The Crossroads of the World (6671 Sunset Boulevard, at Las Palmas Avenue) is a 1930s landmark that signals its worldliness with a revolving globe atop a 60-foot tower. Designed by architect Robert V. Derrah and opened in 1936, the place resembles a sleek, Art Deco ship, supposedly traveling 'round the world to the various ports o' call that surround it—retail buildings in Italian, French, Spanish, Moorish, and Turkish styles. The first "shopping mall" of its time, it's more of a curiosity today, with office space but nothing much to draw shoppers. Nonetheless, it was declared a historic cultural monument in 1974. The movie *L.A. Confidential* (1997) used it as the location for the offices of the scandal magazine published by Danny De Vito's character.

Next door is a building many consider more beautiful—the Catholic Church of the Blessed Sacrament, built in 1928. Bing Crosby married Dixie Lee here in 1930.

The low-slung offices at 6715 Sunset for many years housed the *Hollywood Reporter*, the movie business trade paper started by publisher Billy Wilkerson in 1930. The *Reporter* moved out in the early 1990s for "trade paper row" on Wilshire Boulevard, west of Highland Avenue, and the Sunset offices now house the *L.A. Weekly*, an alternative newspaper.

The remnants of the original movie studios built by Chaplin are nearby, although they're easy to miss at the crowded, fast-food-heavy corner of Sunset and La Brea Avenue. Chaplin erected his palatial home and workplace at 1416 North La Brea in 1919, after breaking free of Mack Sennett and joining D.W. Griffith, Mary Pickford, and Douglas Fairbanks to create United Artists. The film business was still viewed unfavorably by locals, so Chaplin used the Tudor style to cloak his operation as a residential-looking development that blended

into the landscape.

Beginning in 1966, the former Chaplin studios became the home of A&M Records, the hit label founded by Herb Alpert and Jerry Moss. The premises are still in creative hands as the home of puppet animators Jim Henson Productions, whose mascot Kermit the Frog tips his hat to passers-by from the roof.

Further west is the former site of Schwab's Drugstore at the corner of Sunset and Crescent Heights boulevards, now a splashy entertainment and shopping complex anchored by the Virgin Megastore, a cavernous emporium for CDs, videotapes, and DVDs. The flagship West Coast store has a famously deep selection, plus an adjacent bookstore heavy on arts-related titles. Buzz coffeehouse next door is great for people watching, as is the bar at Wolfgang Puck's restaurant. The Laemmle's Sunset 5 multiplex upstairs focuses on art-house and specialty independent films, catering to an

avid local audience, including gays and lesbians. The chain was founded by the same Carl Laemmle who started Universal Pictures at the corner of Sunset and Gower.

Schwab's, a longtime hangout for actors idling away the time between jobs, remained on the corner until 1987, although its long soda fountain counter disappeared sometime in the 1950s. Lana Turner was discovered at a different malt shop, yet starstruck hopefuls patronized this one just the same. One of the all-time great American songs was born here, when composer Harold Arlen sat at the counter late one night to scribble down the melody to "Somewhere Over the Rainbow." Schwab's

was also featured briefly in the movie *Sunset Boulevard*, when William Holden, out for a night on the town in his gigolo threads and Gloria Swanson's car, nips in to say hello to some struggling actor pals.

On the same side of Sunset, across Crescent Heights where a Washington Mutual Bank now fronts a strip mall, is the spot where the storied Garden of Allah apartments once stood and thrived for decades as a playground of the stars and literati.

Silent film star Alla Nazimova, a Russ-

THE GARDEN OF ALLAH
HOTEL AND VILLAS
8152 SUNSET BOULEVARD · · HOLLYWOOD, CALIF

banana, bamboo, and cedar.

Over the years, residents included F. Scott Fitzgerald, Sheilah Graham, Dorothy Parker, Robert Benchley, Ernest Hemingway, Clark Gable, Erroll Flynn, Tallulah Bankhead, Frank Sinatra, Ava Gardner, and others. The courtyard witnessed frivolity and debauchery of all varieties, along with robbery, murder, drunkenness, and divorce, amid which various works of literature and theater were occasionally written and rehearsed.

Nazimova died in 1945 but the bungalow courts staggered on, until a bank, Lytton Savings and Loan, bought the grounds to build its home office. The villa was razed in 1959—but not before a final party, to which 350 guests were invited but 1,000 showed up. The pool was full of empty liquor bottles by midnight, and Flynn's former bed was much fought over at an auction. For years, a model of the bungalow courts could be viewed within the bank now standing there, but even that has since been stored out of sight.

ian émigré, found her fortunes fading as the silent era gave way to the talkies and decid-

·····················

The Garden of Allah apartment complex, where Hollywood stories were written and lived out. Opposite, above: The Charlie Chaplin studios on La Brea, photographed in 1921 after a rare snowfall. Opposite, below: Schwab's drugstore, site of the fabled counter.

ed in 1927 to sustain herself by turning her private villa into a courtyard-style rental complex. The Garden of Allah was exotic, to say the least. Twenty-five Mediterranean bungalows surrounded the swimming pool, the largest in Hollywood and shaped like the Black Sea from Nazimova's homeland. The lush landscaping included ferns, citrus,

Clubland East

Hollywood today is the home of a thriving and diverse nightclub scene that picked up steam in the late 1990s and continues to evolve, frequently yielding hot spots for dancing, dining, and live music that wax and wane in favor among the fickle denizens of the night.

The Cahuenga corridor between Sunset and Hollywood boulevards became an "in" spot with a row of trendy clubs like the Beauty Bar, a Manhattan spinoff that mixes manicures with libations; the Burgundy Room; the Room; the Hotel Cafe, a coffeehouse featuring live jazz and poets; and the Catalina Bar & Grill, an upscale mainstay for live jazz. Just south of Sunset, the former headquarters of the *Variety* trade paper (which long ago moved to Wilshire Boulevard) was converted into an upscale supper club, the Sunset Room, in the 1990s.

On nearby Vine Street is Daddy's, a sleek hipster watering hole, and Deep, a cabaret-like space with a sexy vibe and provocative live shows. Older bars like Boardner's, tucked into side streets and back alleys, compete with exotic one-night-a-week theme nights at intimate dives to capture the favor of nighttime players who venture east from the Sunset Strip.

Alma Mater of the Stars

It's hard to miss Hollywood High School, whose 13-acre campus dominates an entire block at the corner of Sunset Boulevard and Highland Avenue.

From this campus, in 1936, a ravishing sophomore new to town named Judy Turner cut a typing class and ran across the street for a soda at the Top Hat Cafe. Billy Wilkerson, publisher of the *Hollywood Reporter*, was there and asked if she'd like to be in pictures. "I don't know, I'll have to ask my mother," was Judy's reply. Wilkerson made the right introductions for the 15-year-old, who went on to become movie star Lana Turner. Studio publicists altered the story to have the discovery take place at nearby and better-known Schwabs Drugstore, and a legend was born.

But Hollywood High was already well known. Established in 1905 as the area's first public high school, it developed a lively drama department and became

....

Dancers perform at Deep, a new Hollywood hot spot. Opposite: Hollywood High School circa 1905, shortly after the campus opened.

Hollywood's go-to talent pool for fresh, young performers. Stars such as Mickey Rooney and Judy Garland were already famous when they enrolled there, in between movie productions, around the same time Lana appeared. Mickey is remembered as a showboat who used to pull his light blue convertible right onto the lawn, while Garland was quieter and a more dedicated student.

The campus is the alma mater of dozens of television and movie stars, including John Ritter, who was student body president in 1966; Carol Burnett, who edited the school newspaper; Swoozie Kurtz; Barbara Hershey; and David Carradine. The names of dozens of entertainment alumni are displayed on stars painted onto the school's interior walls. The school has also bred talented grads apart from show business, including Norman Chandler, who was publisher of the *Los Angeles Times*; William Shockley, a Nobel Prize winner for chemistry; and Episcopal Bishop James J. Pike. A hit album was recorded live in the school's auditorium in 1979 by British new wave pop artist Elvis Costello.

In the 1970s and 1980s, Hollywood suffered an influx of prostitution and drug dealing, along with motels catering to such activities, creating no small amount of tension in the area around the campus. One prostitute was quoted in the Hollywood High newspaper complaining that her noontime customers were being scared off by students spilling out onto Sunset Boulevard during lunch hour.

In more recent years, the area has been somewhat cleaned up, but low-rent motels and a drug rehabilitation clinic stand directly across from the school.

Through it all, resilient students soldier on. Now designated a performing arts magnet site, the school boasts a revitalized music program, a marching band that performs in the annual Hollywood Christmas parade, and a drama department that stages five productions a year. And on occasion, talent scouts join an audience, hoping to discover a star.

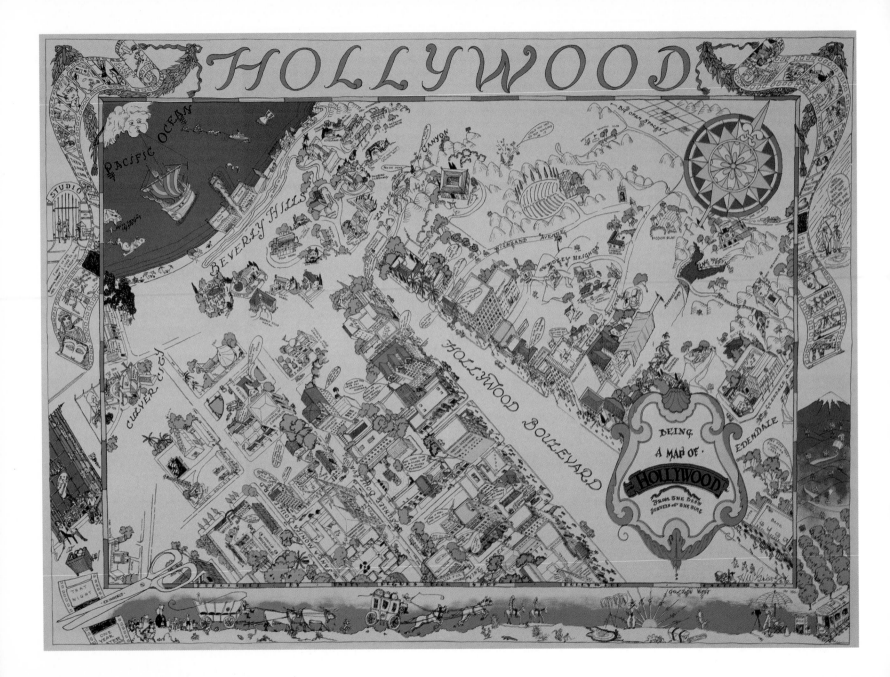

Hollywood Boulevard

In the 1920s, when Los Angeles' infamous sprawl dragged the city westward, Hollywood Boulevard became the hot spot for a new style of wining, dining, shopping, and merrymaking. The boulevard brimmed with celebrity sightings, exotic architecture, and magical movie palaces whose searchlights raked the sky to announce glitzy premieres.

A remarkable 80 percent of the buildings that existed on Hollywood Boulevard in the 1930s have survived. (The 13-block stretch between Argyle and La Brea avenues was declared a national historic district in 1985 in recognition of its high concentration of significant Art Deco architecture.) Dozens of these buildings are being rejuvenated as part of a massive community redevelopment, including the 1927 former Broadway department store at Hollywood and Vine Street, and the Equitable building across the street, which will soon house a retro diner and hip lounge. And with the

....
Hollywood Boulevard's famous sidewalk; Opposite: Illustrated street map of Hollywood, circa 1926.

revival of such showplaces as the El Capitan, Egyptian, and Pantages theaters, construction of a major retail and dining complex at Hollywood and Highland Avenue, and the return of the Academy Awards to a permanent Hollywood home, the stage is set for the area to enjoy a comeback.

Perhaps the best way to become familiar with the street's landmarks and cultural background is to take the self-guided walking tour of the 15 blocks along the boulevard between Gower Street and Sycamore Avenue. Forty-six orange signs mark the route, pointing out significant sites and architecture.

Underfoot is the iconic Walk of Fame, with its twinkling pinkish-coral stars laid into gray terrazzo squares to honor present and past celebrities of the movie, television, radio, and recording industries. The stars are doled out by a committee of the Hollywood Chamber of Commerce, which created the tourist attraction in 1961. Some honorees lobby hard for the privilege; others are scarcely interested. Usually the recipient's studio or agent pays for the star, which costs $15,000. Some of the names mystify completely—they represent a grasp for immortality that succeeded only here—and tourists remain puzzled by their existence. Among the true legends, a few favorites can be found clustered together: Charlie Chaplin (at 6751 Hollywood Boulevard), Marilyn Monroe (at 6774), and Elvis Presley (at 6777).

wet concrete in the theater's forecourt. Mary Pickford and Douglas Fairbanks were the first to cooperate. The courtyard quickly became a tourist attraction.

Today, it's fun to note how the concrete-embedded messages of the early stars denote the clubby, small-town atmosphere of Hollywood at the time. ("To my friend Grauman, lots of luck," wrote cowboy actor William Hart), and how the tiny high heels of stars like Pickford (who was less than five feet tall) gave way to the bare feet of contemporary free spirit Susan Sarandon. Now owned by the Mann's chain, the theater remains a key venue for red-carpet celebrity premieres and draws charged-up first-night audiences.

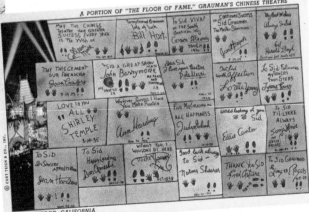

Another major tourist attraction, Grauman's Chinese Theatre (6925 Hollywood Boulevard, east of Orange Avenue), still stands where it was built in 1927 by showman Sid Grauman, complete with exotic pagodas, temple bells, and Fu dogs—and celebrity imprints. The story goes that Grauman hit on the idea of movie stars leaving their footprints, handprints, and signatures in cement after he accidentally stepped in

Much of the nation got its first glimpse of Hollywood from newsreels or magazine layouts showing the star-studded movie premieres that were born on this street, a promotional concept hatched by Grauman with Otto K. Oleson. An entrepreneur known for his portable "light brigade," Ole-son executed his idea for the sky-sweeping searchlights by mounting a war-surplus, battleship carbon arc lamp on wheels.

The first of these showy premieres took place in 1922 at the Egyptian Theatre (6712 Hollywood Boulevard, west of Las Palmas Avenue), another of Grauman's show-places. The Egyptian, the first of the great theaters erected in Hollywood, featured a palm tree-lined courtyard entry, carved columns, hieroglyphs and sphinxes, reflecting the craze sparked that year by the discovery of King Tut-ankhamen's tomb. Splendidly refurbished in 1998 as the home of the non-profit American Cinematheque, the theater now exhibits classic and special-interest films. Next door, the Pig 'n Whis-tle restaurant was restored to its original 1920s Art Deco glory and reopened in 2001.

The spectacular El Capitan Theatre (at 6834 Hollywood Boulevard, west of Highland Avenue) is an Art Deco gem that opened in 1926 as a live performance venue. It became

the Paramount movie house in 1942. But over the years, it was left to deteriorate. In the late 1980s, the Disney Co. took it over and beautifully restored its baroque, East Indian and Moorish design elements. The theater reopened in 1991 and is a key showplace for Disney premieres. Live pre-show entertainment (during special events) and the dazzling "curtain show" make it a memorable place to attend a movie.

Above: Detail from Egyptian Theatre courtyard. Right: Pig 'n Whistle restaurant logo and detail from restored ceiling above the box office at the El Capitan Theatre. Opposite: Grauman's Chinese Theatre in 1927, the year it opened, and its famous hand- and footprints.

The most stunning of all of Hollywood Boulevard's restored showplaces may be the Pantages Theatre (6233 Hollywood Boulevard), near the historic corner of Hollywood and Vine. Reopened in October 2000 as the home of Disney's hit live musical *The Lion King*, this 1929 treasure boasts a dazzling interior and grand lobby, with two sweeping staircases. The ornate Zigzag Moderne walls and ceiling are gilded with more than 84,000 feet of brass, aluminum, and copper leafing. The $10-million restoration was funded by owner James Nederlander, and easily brings back the glamour of a night out in old Hollywood. The Pantages was designed by architect B. Marcus Priteca as a movie house at the height of the Roaring '20s. The Academy Awards were held there from 1950 to 1960, and Howard Hughes once occupied offices upstairs.

Another historic movie palace—currently dormant—

sits at the corner of Wilcox Avenue and Hollywood. Built by Warner Bros. in 1928 as the company's first West Coast theater, the Warner Pacific (6423-45 Hollywood Boulevard) seated 2,700 and had a 26-rank pipe organ. The Hollywood Pacific chain purchased it in 1968. The blue neon towers, visible for miles around at night, were relit as part of a program to restore historic neon landmarks sponsored by the Community Redevelopment Agency.

At the corner of Hollywood and Highland stands the picturesque archway evoking the Babylonian decor of the *Intolerance* movie set built for D.W. Griffith on Sunset Boulevard in 1916 (see page 69). Flanked by trumpeting elephants, the arch is part of an ambitious new $650-million shopping, hotel, and dining complex that is anchored by a Metro Rail subway station and the 3,300-seat Kodak Theatre, built as the permanent new home of the Academy Awards ceremony.

Beginning in March 2002, the $94-million theater is slated to bring the orgy of Oscar-giving back to Hollywood for the first time since 1960. The post-ceremony Governors Ball is being be held in a 25,000-square-foot ballroom atop the entryway, designed to recall the Art Deco glamour of 1929, when the awards were first held.

the 12-story Hollywood Roosevelt Hotel (7000 Hollywood Boulevard, at Orange Avenue), whose 1927 opening signified confidence that the movie industry was here to stay and would bring to town a steady stream of wealthy clientele. The first Academy Awards were held in a ballroom of the Spanish Colonial Revival structure. The second-floor balcony overlooking the lobby offers a free mini-museum of Hollywood history, with photographs and ephemera detailing the area's early years and development. Stories about this atmospheric landmark abound, including one that says Shirley Temple was taught to tap dance on the lobby staircase by Bill "Bojangles" Robinson for their famous movie scene together. Another says the ghost of Montgomery Clift haunts Room 928, where he can sometimes be heard blowing his bugle. Regardless, the well-located hotel features a civilized lobby for drinking and relaxing, plus nightly entertainment at the Cinegrill

A visitors' information center in the Hollywood & Highland entertainment complex will open in 2002 and offer free brochures, maps, and other guidance.

The intersection of Hollywood and Highland was an important spot in the community long ago. For more than 50 years, the corner was the site of the Hollywood Hotel, the community's first great lodging house when it was built in 1903, and the inn of choice for the early film colony. Rudolph Valentino honeymooned here with his first bride, Jean Acker. Gossip maven Louella Parsons made it nationally famous by broadcasting her radio show from the lobby. But the hotel fell to the wrecking ball in 1956.

A few blocks west stands

Above: Outdoor courtyard of the modern Hollywood & Highland complex, with elephants copied from the Babylon set of *Intolerance*. Below: Interior of the Kodak Theatre, the new home of the Academy Awards ceremony. Opposite: Stunning Art Deco interior of the Pantages, as originally designed in 1929.

supper club, where chanteuse Eartha Kitt and songman Jimmy Webb have performed, and where part of *The Fabulous Baker Boys* (1989) was filmed.

The literary lore of Hollywood can be traced to various historic locales, including Musso & Frank Grill (6667 Hollywood Boulevard) the area's oldest eatery, dating back to 1919. In the 1930s and 1940s, such writers as William Faulkner, Nathaniel West, Raymond Chandler, and William Saroyan held court here, bending their elbows at the bar to anesthetize themselves against the Hollywood barbarians for whom they were writing scripts. Still thriving, the restaurant is old school in every way, from the ancient waiters and red booths to a menu that hasn't changed much in decades.

Nearby on Ivar Avenue, half a block north of Hollywood Boulevard, is the storied Knickerbocker Hotel, where Faulkner stayed while toiling by day on the screenplay for Howard Hawk's *Road To Glory* (1936) and writing the novel *Absalom, Absalom!* (1936) by night. Director Griffith was living here in 1948 when he drew his last breath in the lobby before succumbing to a cerebral hemorrhage. Presley stayed at the hotel in 1956 during the making of his first Hollywood movie, *Love Me Tender*. It's

since been converted into residential housing for seniors.

A block farther up Ivar Avenue stands another literary shrine—the red-brick Parva Sed-Apta apartments (1817 North Ivar), where West lived while writing his dark, unsettling Hollywood novel *The Day Of the Locust* (1939). The white apartment house nearby at 1851 North Ivar was the movie locale where hack screenwriter Joe Gillis (William Holden) lived while tapping out stories before he stumbled into Norma Desmond's nightmare world in *Sunset Boulevard* (1950).

Back on the boulevard, the southwest corner of Hollywood and Cahuenga has been designated Raymond Chandler Square. The 1921 structure here, informally known as "the Cahuenga building" in Chandler's era, was the workplace the writer gave his fictional detective, Philip Marlowe, who kept an office on the sixth floor. The building's architects, John and Donald Parkinson, also designed the landmark Bullock's Wilshire building, another Chandler favorite. Careful readers will note that Marlowe left his shoe leather all over Hollywood. He delighted in using his razor-sharp wit to let the air out of the place.

••••••••••••••••••••

Hollywood's oldest restaurant, circa its 1919 opening year. The boulevard's first movie palace, the Egyptian, was constructed practically across the street in 1922.

Boulevard of Broken Dreams

For decades, particularly in the 1970s and 1980s, the once grand streets of Hollywood were all but given up for lost. Hollywood Boulevard and its star-studded sidewalks became to some degree a *Day of the Locust* sideshow, a Fellini-esque runway for junkies and drifters, hookers and homeless teens, mixed with baffled tourists not likely to return.

What became of the glamorous and wholesome-seeming era when Mickey Rooney and Judy Garland attended Hollywood High on Sunset, and stars such as Clark Gable and Marlene Dietrich shopped at the Broadway department store on Hollywood Boulevard?

Changes upon changes had battered the area, some spawned by the inevitable tides of time, economics, and sprawling development, others by changing laws and changing social mores.

By the 1950s, most of the movie studios had left Hollywood, taking with them the stars and good jobs that had nourished upscale businesses and restaurants. The era of live radio that had enlivened the scene in the 1930s and 1940s was over, too, replaced by television, whose programs often originated from relocated studios in the San Fernando Valley and elsewhere.

The freeways were built—a major development that made it possible for workers to live anywhere and commute to the jobs remaining in Hollywood more swiftly (in theory) than had previously been possible. With the studios largely gone, and a new freeway (named "The Hollywood" for the community it barrels through), the residential composition of old Hollywood changed. Families with dreams of suburban nirvana were lured northward into the San Fernando Valley, and blocks of sweet bungalows that once housed them were knocked down. The replacements were cheap stucco apartments that attracted a more transient population as well as multitudes of struggling immigrants who made the neighborhoods south of Sunset their own.

A key school redistricting in 1968 intensified the shift, as students in upscale Hollywood neighborhoods were channeled to schools in nearby sections of the San Fernando Valley. Until that year, English had been the first language of 98 percent of the student body of Hollywood High School. Waves of immigration brought in a new student body, and by the 1990s the historic school was accommodating students from 76 countries.

Equally significant to Hollywood's central business district was a series of late 1960s court rulings on obscenity that loosened restrictions on what could be shown in movie theaters. Suddenly, rundown Hollywood theaters that had been subsisting on art-house fare were doing, relatively speaking, boffo box office with once-banned adult movies. The "XXX" business spread, bringing in such ancillary operations as strip bars, massage parlors, and prostitution.

At the same time, youth culture was exploding in the clubs along the Sunset Strip, making Hollywood a magnet for long-haired flower children, trippers, hustlers and seekers. Many were drug users or runaways, bringing with them panhandling, prostitution, and crime.

In the late 1980s, the collapse of the Southern California aerospace industry triggered an area-wide economic recession. Hollywood sank into a prolonged funk. Its resurgence today is a tribute to the persistence of merchants, politicians, preservationists, die-hard boosters, and profit-hungry developers who pushed a full-scale redevelopment program in the mid-1990s. Hollywood is poised for the same tawdry-to-wholesome transformation that Times Square in Manhattan has experienced—a potential "Hollywood ending" of its own. Ⓢ

Check it out: Central Hollywood

Food and Drink

Pinot Hollywood, 1448 North Gower Street, (323) 461-8800. Power lunch/dinner spot for film colony on site of old Columbia commissary, with martini bar, celebrity chef Joachim Splichal.

Roscoe's House of Chicken and Waffles, 1541 North Gower Street, (323) 466-7453. Soul food, waffles in super-popular setting.

Frolic Room, 6245 Hollywood Boulevard (just east of Vine), (323) 462-5890. Bukowski-style barflies, slumming rock stars, and Pantages looky-loos mingle in this cozy dive, which features a 1963 Al Hirschfeld celebrity mural.

Musso & Frank Grill, 6667 Hollywood Boulevard, (323) 467-7788. Classic Hollywood atmosphere and vintage waiters in area's oldest restaurant and bar, since 1919.

Pig 'n Whistle, 6714 Hollywood Boulevard, (323) 463-0000. Restored 1927 bistro, bar. Back room redefines "intimate" dining by offering canopied beds alongside tables. Adjacent to Egyptian Theatre.

Miceli's, 1646 North Las Palmas Avenue, (323) 466-3438. Warm, casual Italian restaurant, lost-in-time atmosphere, red-checked table cloths, old-school menu, hanging chianti bottles. Piano bar, singing.

Boardner's, 1652 North Cherokee Avenue, (323) 462-9621. Since the 1940s, comfortable, unpretentious watering hole with red leather booths. Also, theme nights with DJs, dancing.

Les Deux Cafes, 1638 North Las Palmas Avenue, (323) 465-0509. Sensual, low-lit hideaway for celebs and stylish set. French cuisine, deep wine list.

The Sunset Room, 1430 North Cahuenga Boulevard, (323) 463-0004. Celebrity sightings, French-Asian cuisine in elegant, happening supper club.

Cat & Fiddle Pub, 6530 Sunset Boulevard, (323) 468-3800. Open-air courtyard, British pub fare, live music. Long-time magnet for ex-pat Brits and rockers.

Green Room, 6752 Hollywood Boulevard, (323) 860-0775. Sandwich and coffee shop featuring live acoustic music.

360 Restaurant and Lounge, 6290 Sunset Boulevard, (323) 871-2995. 360-degree view from atop tower at Hollywood Boulevard and Vine Street in upscale restaurant, bar.

Catalina Bar & Grill, 1640 North Cahuenga Boulevard, (323) 466- 2210. Long-time premiere jazz spot and supper club.

The Room, 1626 North Cahuenga Boulevard, (323) 462-7196. Trendy, back-alley boite for drinking, grooving while DJs spin soulful sounds.

Beauty Bar, 1638 North Cahuenga Boulevard, (323) 464-7676. Fun, sparkly cocktail spot offering manicures and makeovers amid vintage salon chairs and fixtures.

Burgundy Room, 1621 1/2 North Cahuenga Boulevard, (323) 465-7530. Dark, intimate drinking spot, where bar is occasionally set afire for the entertainment of all.

The Palace, 1735 North Vine Street, (323) 462-3000. Live music, dance events in historic Old Hollywood venue.

Specialty Shopping

The Daily Planet Bookstore, 5931 1/2 Franklin Avenue (at Tamarind Avenue), (323) 957-0061. Stimulating selection of books, periodicals, gifts at shop anchoring Franklin's East Village-style strip.

Amoeba Music, 6400 Sunset Boulevard, (323) 245-6400. Vast selection of new and used CDs, adjacent to Cinerama Dome.

Samuel French Theatre & Film Bookshop, 7623 Sunset Boulevard, (323) 876-0570. Theatrical plays, screenplays, books, and materials for actors and writers.

Guitar Alley, corner of Sunset Boulevard and Gardner Street. World's largest collection of guitar shops, including Valdez Guitar, Freedom Guitar, Sunset Custom Guitars, Guitars R Us, Guitar Center, many others. Developed mainly during 1980s to cater to L.A.'s burgeoning rock 'n' roll scene and nearby Musician's Institute of Hollywood.

Special Events and Tours

American Film Institute's Los Angeles International Film Festival. Annual event draws top international filmmakers, newest films from around the world. Presented at historic Egyptian Theatre and other venues for 10 days in early November. Information: (323) 856-7707 or www.afi.com.

Hollywood Christmas Parade. Televised event held annually on the Sunday after Thanksgiving, 6-8 p.m., on Hollywood and Sunset boulevards, commencing in front of the Chinese Theatre. First held in 1928, with live reindeer pulling sleigh. Gene Autry's hit Christmas tune "Here Comes Santa Claus" was inspired in 1946 when he listened to the shouts of children while riding his horse, Champion, in the parade.

Hollywood Farmers Market. 8 a.m. to 1 p.m. Sundays on Ivar Avenue between Sunset and Hollywood boulevards. Fresh produce from around the state, flowers, plants, live music, gourmet tamales, crafts, people-watching, celebrity-spotting.

Paramount Pictures studio tours, 5555 Melrose Avenue, (323) 956-1777. Two-hour walking tour combines historical look at Hollywood's last remaining major studio with visits to soundstages of current TV shows and films. Tours depart hourly from 9 a.m. to 2 p.m., Monday through Friday. $15 per person.

Grave Line Tours, (816) 333-2577. Tours depart at 9:30 a.m. daily from Orchid Street and Hollywood Boulevard, near the Chinese Theatre. Darker side of Hollywood explored in coach tours focusing on scandal, murder, and death sites. $44 per person.

....

Sampling axes at Hollywood's Guitar Center. Opposite: The Frolic Room, next door to the Pantages Theatre.

On Location

Many classic movies,

including *Sunset Boulevard, Chinatown,* and *A Star Is Born,* have captured both the mythology and the reality of the boulevard of dreams.

Most enduring, perhaps, is the picture actually named for the street—Billy Wilder's divinely decadent Hollywood tragedy about a forgotten film star (Gloria Swanson) who snares a desperate screenwriter (William Holden) in her web of self-delusion.

The 1950 black-and-white *film noir* begins with Joe Gillis (Holden) floating dead in the swimming pool of the decaying mansion at 10086 Sunset Boulevard, then flashes back to earlier, when a car chase down Sunset to avoid bill collectors first led the writer to this fatal address. The film goes on to include real-life locales, such as Schwab's, the fabled malt shop that stood at Sunset and Crescent Heights boulevards until 1983, and the ornate entrance gates at Paramount Pictures, which still stand within the expanded studio property.

No use trying to spot the mansion, however, among the many candidates in the Beverly Hills section of Sunset—it was actually located on Wilshire Boulevard, on the corner at 641 Irving Street. The residence of Mrs. J. Paul Getty at the time of filming, the place was torn down in 1957. Its swimming pool, built expressly for *Sunset Boulevard,* was used again for a climactic scene in the movie *Rebel Without a Cause* (1955).

The harsh light that Wilder and cowriter Charles Brackett shone on the film world's glamorous pretensions made *Sunset Boulevard* shocking for its time; nevertheless, it was nominated for 11 Academy

....

Actress Nancy Olson helps a stricken William Holden in the 1950 thriller *Union Station,* shot at the namesake train depot. Opposite, left: Poster from the 1950 classic named for the street, again featuring Holden, with famous opening scene shown at bottom. Opposite, right: Jack Nicholson, as private eye Jake Gittes, at work at Echo Park Lake in Roman Polanski's *Chinatown* (1974).

Awards, and won for best screenplay, art direction, and score.

Andrew Lloyd Webber's stage musical version, launched in London in 1993, became a huge success, with its cast album and attendant publicity doing much to make the name "Sunset Boulevard" famous around the world.

Sites on or near Sunset Boulevard were also important in *Chinatown,* another movie that did much to create the mythology of Los Angeles. Echo Park Lake, Stone Canyon Reservoir in Bel-Air, the old Eastern Star retirement home in Brentwood, and, of course, Chinatown itself (in the movie's final

scene) were the locations for key moments in the Oscar-winning modern-day *film noir*. The 1974 movie, directed by Roman Polanski from a screenplay by Robert Towne, starred Jack Nicholson as a 1940s private eye investigating the murder of the city's water commissioner for his widow (Faye Dunaway).

Sunset Boulevard and its landmarks and neighborhoods have played roles in scores of other movies.

The same year William Holden starred in *Sunset Boulevard*, he played the lead in *Union Station*, a well-regarded suspense thriller about the hunt for the kidnapper of a blind girl, set largely against the backdrop of the then-bustling

train station.

The original version of the thrice-filmed romantic tragedy *A Star Is Born* (1937, with Janet Gaynor and Fredric March), about a starlet whose career takes off just as that of her older lover fades, captures the glamour of the Sunset Strip in its 1930s heyday with scenes shot at the Trocadero nightclub.

The 1951 film noir *The Strip*, starring Mickey Rooney, opens with a sweeping overhead pan of its namesake, near the Chateau Marmont, and features a montage of the era's hot night spots.

Echo Park, writ-

ten by Michael Ventura and released in 1986, captures the particular vibe of that hillside community as experienced by a trio of struggling artists (Tom Hulce, Susan Dey, and Michael Bowen).

And then there's the 1967 exploitation picture *Riot on Sunset Strip*, a camp classic that captures the hostility of the era's adults and authority figures toward the hippie menace. American International Pictures pumped out the piece to capitalize on headlines following real-life scuffles on the Strip. The low-budgeter—about a cop (Aldo Ray) whose bad-girl daughter (Mimsy Farmer) takes up with the dope-smokers—features the hair, fashions, and music of the era, and still turns up at cult film festivals celebrating the 1960s. ⑤

The Sunset Strip

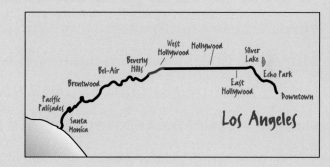

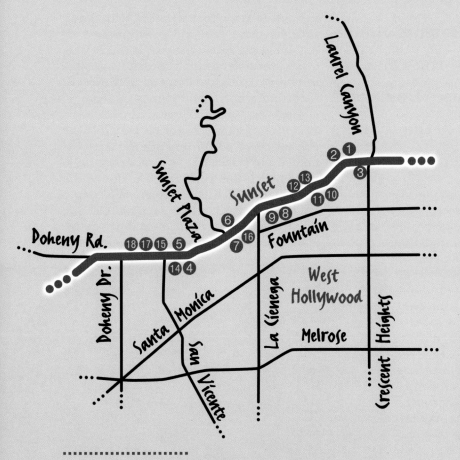

1. **Chateau Marmont Hotel**
2. **Miyagi's restaurant/ site of Players Club**
3. **Site of Pandora's Box nightclub**
4. **Book Soup**
5. **Tower Records**
6. **Sunset Plaza**
7. **Site of Trocadero nightclub**
8. **House of Blues**
9. **Mondrian Hotel/Skybar**
10. **Standard Hotel**
11. **Argyle Hotel/Fenix**
12. **Comedy Store/ site of Ciro's nightclub**
13. **Hyatt House Hotel**
14. **Viper Room**
15. **Whisky a Go-Go**
16. **Site of Mocambo nightclub**
17. **The Roxy**
18. **Rainbow Bar & Grill**

Opposite: The loud, lively energy of the Sunset Strip, looking east from Tower Records.

Just beyond Crescent Heights Boulevard, where the French Normandie tower of the Chateau Marmont hotel looms up against the hills, Sunset Boulevard alchemizes into the fabled Sunset Strip. Here, in the 1.7-mile stretch between Crescent Heights and Doheny Drive, the

boulevard becomes twisty and sensual, the Hollywood hills nudging down against it on one side, an intoxicating panorama of city lights spread out below it on the other. The street's energy becomes louder, its lore thicker and more varied, as a blur of night-clubs, hotels, restaurants, boutiques, and those famous outsized billboards pass by.

Here, Sunset Boulevard enters the city of West Hollywood, sometimes called "the Creative City" thanks to its high concentration of residents employed in the worlds of art, design, film, and television. Known also as "the Gay Camelot," West Hollywood elected the first city council in the nation with an openly gay majority shortly after it was incorporated in 1984. A great many of its 37,000 residents are gays and lesbians, mixed with straights and popula-

tions of Jewish retirees and Russian immigrants. West Hollywood's true personality—and the center of its gay life—is found south of Sunset among the abundant cafes, shops, and theaters of Santa Monica Boulevard, which was recently widened and beautified to foster an even livelier sidewalk culture.

The Sunset Strip, on the other hand, is an entity unto itself—a scene that belongs not so much to the neighborhood as to the world. This is where promoters and restaurateurs play out their pop culture dreams; where stars make splashy entrances or take tragic final exits; where lasting memories

are made for every kind of club-goer, tourist, music fan, and scene-maker. By day, amid the roaring traffic of this relentlessly traversed asphalt, the office towers of the Strip buzz with the business of record and movie companies, managers, and agents. Venerable restaurants like the French culinary temple Le Dome (8720 Sunset) host power lunches for the well-heeled old guard of show business, who remember when the Strip was one of the few places in L.A. where one could find a good restaurant. Right alongside them, longhaired rockers drift into divey coffee shops for afternoon breakfasts, or pound

the sidewalks past tattoo parlors and strip clubs putting up flyers for their gigs.

The enormous new Sunset Millennium project under construction just west of La Cienega Boulevard will soon change the retail character of the Strip. But the stretch does have its shopping traditions. One is attending a book signing or simply browsing at Book Soup (8818 Sunset), a literary destination for the last 25 years. Another is trolling for CDs at the flagship Tower Records (8801 Sunset, with video and classical outlets across the street), a magnet for music lovers since 1970 and the site of many

....

Above: Swank shopping among the boutiques of Sunset Plaza. Right: Book Soup, the longtime literary hub of the Strip. Opposite: Tower Records, in the days of the vinyl LP.

a midnight lineup for hot new releases or in-store appearances by recording artists.

High-end shopping is practiced among the boutiques of the Sunset Plaza area (8591-8720 Sunset, just west of La Cienega, on both sides of the street), where excess money can be burnt up efficiently at clothing and jewelry stores like Billy Martin's, Nicole Miller, Herve Leger Paris, Dolce & Gabana, and Hugo Boss. Sunset Plaza cultivates an ambience that's part European sidewalk bistro scene, part Rodeo Drive. The tables in front of cafes like Clafoutis and Chin Chin are always taken, crowded with those who tend to wear Rolex

watches and Gucci loafers with no socks, and who speak either in showbiz parlance or in Italian, Arabic, or French. It's the kind of scene where a drop-dead gorgeous model will take a calculated stroll across the street just to watch the traffic stop. And the forks. And the cell-phone conversations.

In the dark, the Strip morphs into a different beast. Long the nexus of pop culture and nightlife in Los Angeles, this stretch of Sunset has seen it all, from the fabled era of the 1930s and 1940s, when glamorous night-clubs and restaurants first opened here, to the peace-and-love carnival of the 1960s rock revolution, all the way through the dol-

drums of the late 1980s, as the hard-rock and heavy-metal scene wound down.

With the economic boom of the 1990s, a new era announced itself as a bold generation of hoteliers, restaurateurs, and music impresarios colonized old landmarks. Bringing playfulness, whimsy, and visual extravagance to the party, they created new spaces to see and be seen. Once again the Strip on a summer weekend was roaring, peaking, awash with actors and models sipping $10 cocktails; gawking cruisers and tourists; and strutters and players displaying their assets, material and otherwise. Celebrities have invested in many of the hot spots and drop by frequently to

join the party or to give impromptu shows on intimate club stages.

A good place to start a tour is at the House of Blues (8430 Sunset), a club many credit with reviving the energy of the Strip. In May 1994, impresario Isaac Tigrett took a chance on the corner of Sunset and North Olive Drive, investing $9 million in a three-

story corrugated metal shack that resembles a Mississippi Delta-style roadhouse in Disneyland. He filled it with folk art by "outsider" artists like the Reverend Howard Finster, and embarked on an adventurous booking policy that encompasses blues with roots rock, world music, country, rap, soul, and emerging talents.

Like other promoters who would set the pace for the Strip renaissance, Tigrett created a space that felt special, a place so visually compelling that just being there was worth the price of admission. The House of Blues also offered great sound; great sight lines; and the exclusive upstairs Foundation Room, a plush, East

Indian-themed VIP area that had celebs like Bruce Springsteen, Bonnie Raitt, Madonna, and Prince lining up to get in the first year. Detractors still complain about the pushy bouncers and the constant chattering of bar patrons, and neighbors have pitched a fit about noise and parking, but since the mid-1990s the party on the Strip has been back on and the House of Blues helped start it up.

The success of the reincarnated Mondrian Hotel (8440 Sunset, directly across Olive Street adjacent to the House of Blues) has helped make the corner of Sunset and Olive white-hot since the mid-1990s. Conceived by hotelier Ian Schrager with French architect Philippe Starck, it presents the hotel lobby as a theatrical space that exudes airy, sensual glamour with a touch of whimsy—a play land for the senses and the id.

Incongruous 30-foot mahogany doors flank the valet entrance of the Mondrian, like something out of *Alice in Wonderland*. Inside, all is shimmering and sleek. A thin bar of light projects a faux carpet onto the floor;

• • • • • • • • • • • • • • • • • • • •

The front desk at the super-hip Standard hotel doubles as a DJ booth. Opposite: A stretch limo swoops past the rustic-looking House of Blues.

the elevator bank is encased in a glowing cube; a 60-foot cocktail bar sits free-standing in the room, illuminated from within. Through the lobby and toward the back, a trendy fusion restaurant called Asia de Cuba has become a loud, lively instant hit. On its patio, waiters swivel their way around enormous flowerpots that preside over the intoxicating nighttime view of glittering West Hollywood. Adjacent to the restaurant is the Skybar, an erotic dream of a poolside California evening, where saronged servers ferry cocktails to black-clad hipsters lounging on pillow mattresses or oversized cane chairs. Hotel guests have automatic entrance; others must apply at the velvet rope.

Until Schrager came in and spent $17 million, reopening the place late in 1996, the

Mondrian was a fairly ordinary hotel done up in red, yellow, and blue and named for a mural in its lobby by the Dutch painter. What a transformation, after starting life as an apartment house in 1959.

A short walk to the east, another hotel is a magnet for scene-makers of a younger stripe. The lobby at the Standard (8300 Sunset) turns into a rave by night, with a DJ taking over the front desk to spin records for bobbing, whirling dancers. One needn't be a hotel guest to hang out in this party space, which by day resembles a Mod 1960s rumpus room, with a conversation pit, white shag carpeting, chrome Arco lamps, and Baleri egg-shaped chairs. You half expect Austin Powers to bound in enthusing, "Groovy, baby!" A nearly nude model naps in a modified fish tank behind the front desk, and elsewhere in the lobby a shimmering wall plays high-concept fine-art videos. Out by the pool, when there's not a video shoot or a magazine interview in progress, a performance artist "mows" the electric blue Astro Turf.

With rooms starting at $99, the Standard pitches itself to young people with more pop culture savvy than cash. Its sign is hung upside down on an undulating white facade, and the name is ironic, since

The Big Picture

What neon is to Las Vegas, giant billboards are to the Sunset Strip.

Unique, indelible pieces of the skyline—proclamations that this is no ordinary zone, but a place where life is lived in the fast lane, where youth, style, fame, and the entertainment industry are top priorities—the oversized billboards hoist the ego and id of career-crazed Hollywood into the sky for all to see.

For decades they've taken the temperature of the boulevard and been a kind of insider's code aimed at agents and producers shuttling to and from their Sunset Strip offices, telegraphing that this star is making a comeback in Vegas ... this record company is betting the bank on this new band ... this cable network goes all out to promote its original series. Along the way, they entertain tourists, distract motorists, and have become as much a part of the landscape as the Hollywood sign—all at a cost to advertisers of about $30,000 per billboard per month.

One of the best-remembered billboards went up adjacent to the Chateau Marmont hotel in 1957, advertising the Sahara Hotel in Las Vegas. A fiberglass showgirl dressed in pink stripes twirled on top, her toe poised above a silver dollar. The icon lasted more than 10 years, eventually giving way to a giant cutout of the Marlboro Man. He reigned as the gatekeeper of the Strip until the 1990s, when new rules outlawed billboard advertising for tobacco. A tower-

ing Miller beer bottle now occupies the prime location, blowing its cap at regular intervals and emitting vapors that suggest a cold brew.

The ads helped signal the Strip's demise—when Las Vegas, heavily promoted in Strip billboards, siphoned off most of its allure in the 1950s—and its comeback, when the record industry revitalized the scene in the 1960s and 1970s. In 1967, Elek-

eled underwear for Calvin Klein, and a silicone-enhanced model named Angelyne hyped her wished-for career. In sync with the more recent dot.com boom, the billboards went high tech. Now, at least three jumbo Video-Tron screens display moving ads, animation—even short films—for the further distraction of motorists.

Other innovations include the "tall walls," in which androgynous models strike erotic poses painted 50 feet high on

tra Records started a trend, erecting a giant billboard for the Doors' first album. For the next decade, billboards for rock albums dominated the Strip and proclaimed what was happening. A memorable one advertised the Beatles' *Abbey Road*, with the Fab Four's heads poking up as they crossed the road. Someone cut Paul's head off, helping fuel the rumors that he was dead.

In the 1980s and 1990s, fashion and materialism dominated the outdoor ads. Beverly Hills designer Bijan hawked perfume, "Marky Mark" Wahlberg mod-

the sides of buildings, and playful, self-referential ads such as one for the new Volkswagen Beetle that simply said, "On the list at Skybar." An awards show, the Sunset Strip Billboard Awards, was launched in the year 2000 to draw even more attention and boost creative competition—meaning the images are likely to get even more distracting.

Isn't that going to exacerbate the already dangerous driving conditions? For the most part, motorists seem able to handle it. The

Strip averages 15 to 20 traffic accidents a month, according to the West Hollywod sheriff's substation—but they're usually related to nightclubs and drinking, a Strip tradition long before billboards began to move.

∙∙∙∙∙∙∙∙∙∙∙∙∙∙∙∙∙∙∙∙∙∙∙∙∙

Left: Lucy and Desi "tall walls" typify the playful spirit of Strip billboards. Above, right: Video billboards are the latest thing. Above, left: The big boards seek to mold a range of public tastes and habits. Opposite: The Marlboro Man dominated the Strip for decades, til a ban on tobacco billboards stubbed him out.

the M.O. is to defy convention wherever possible. Formerly the Golden Crest Retirement Home and, before that, the venerable Hollywood Sunset Hotel, where Bob Dylan stayed while playing the Hollywood Bowl in 1965, this piece of prime Sunset Strip real estate claimed its place in the present in 1999. That's when it was remodeled by hotelier Andre Balazs, who also owns the nearby Chateau Marmont.

The Standard's stylish, 24-hour coffee shop—in keeping with the premise that nothing is what it seems—has a renowned chef, Marc Urwand, and serves haute cuisine and cocktails. The lobby includes a Rudy's Barbershop, a spinoff of the one in Seattle that was favored by the late rocker Kurt Cobain. Men as well as women—including Jennifer Lopez, Gloria Estefan, and Rose McGowan—drop by to take advantage of the $19 cuts.

The rooms at the Standard are utilitarian, with trendy touches, but they're beside the point. The point is to join the party in the lobby and maybe catch sight of the hotel's investors, who include Gen-X icons Leonardo DiCaprio and Cameron Diaz. Along with Balazs' wife, modeling agency head Katie Ford, they've helped put this place on the hot list with a steady supply of beautiful people.

The hotel-based side of Sunset Strip night life continues at the Argyle (8358 Sunset), where the Fenix bar and restaurant offers Art Deco glamour, enhanced by George Hurrell photographs of Greta Garbo and Marlene Dietrich. The poolside patio is the place to be on summer nights, sipping cocktails among the vintage plastercast palm trees while enjoying a seductive view of the city lights.

Popularly known as "the wedding cake," the Argyle is widely considered the most beautiful piece of architecture on the Strip. Its pristine 15-story tower was born as an elegant apartment house in 1930, designed by Leland Bryant & Sons in the Streamline Moderne style. At the time, almost no other buildings existed nearby except the Chateau Marmont. Clark Gable moved in here, as did John Wayne in later years. (An oft-repeated story about Wayne keeping a pet steer in his apartment, however, is fictional.)

The elegant apartments enjoyed decades of respectability, but by the late 1960s the Argyle had gone to seed. It closed, and squatters and derelicts moved in until it was scheduled for demolition in the 1970s. Color photos of its sadly tattered condition are on display at

the hotel, testament to the preservationists who saved it. A London-based group bought the property in the mid-1980s and

••••••••••••••••••••

Opposite: The Art Deco-style Sunset Towers (today it's called the Argyle hotel) had the Strip nearly to itself in 1930. The castle-like Chateau Marmont, shown above, rear right, in 1937, was its only significant neighbor.

invested in extensive renovation, down to replicas of the original molding and handcrafted Italian furnishings. The pool terrace and Fenix restaurant were added, and the hotel reopened as the St. James Club in 1986. Movie buffs will recognize its striking entrance and lobby from scenes in *The Player* (1992) and *Get Shorty* (1995). In

1995 the hotel changed hands and was renamed the Argyle, after the men's socks. (The name was chosen in an employee contest.) Today it's a sleek, elegant four-star hotel, favored by such celebs as writer James Ellroy (*L.A. Confidential*) and actor Russell Crowe.

The storied Chateau Marmont (8221 Sunset Boulevard) rises high above the hedges at the eastern edge of the Strip. Legendary in its celebrity lore, it nonetheless cultivates an aura of discretion and privacy—more a hideaway place than a showoff space. Its public areas are few, its restaurant tiny. The lobby, impeccably restored with 1940s-era furnishings, has been known to host red-wine poetry readings that appeal to both literati and glitterati. Breakfast, available to nonguests as well, is served at cane chairs on the lawn patio.

Peak-roofed and Gothic appearing, this imposing 63-room hotel, a knockoff of a castle in France's Loire Valley, started as a luxury apartment building in 1929. The crash of the stock market doused its prospects, so

the place was reborn as a hotel, with eclectic, mismatched furnishings culled from Depression-era Beverly Hills estate sales. The result was a *haute bohemian* feel that the place retains to this day, as a favored haunt of the many writers, musicians, photographers, and actors who make extended stays while working or playing in Hollywood.

Its apartment-style rooms, with their retro kitchens and furnishings, make it a comfortable place to spend weeks, months—even years. And its guest roster reads like a Who's Who of Hollywood, past and present. Greta Garbo was a regular, as was Billy Wilder. Writers Dominick Dunne, Gore Vidal, and Jay McInerney have featured the hotel in their work. Paul Newman and Joanne Woodward ignited their lifelong romance here. James Dean and Natalie Wood met during a script reading for *Rebel Without a Cause* (1955) in Cottage No. 2, then occupied by director Nicholas Ray. Roman Polanski spent his last days in the United States here before fleeing the country to avoid statutory rape charges, and comic John Belushi checked out for good, sadly, at a bungalow up a private, bamboo-lined path after a cocaine and heroin binge in 1982. Robert DeNiro lived in the penthouse for two years, and Howard Hughes lived there for years

long before that, summoning female companions he spotted on the pool deck or the Strip. Jim Morrison lived at the hotel and as various stories go, either fell off the roof or danced drunkenly on it—as represented by Oliver Stone in his movie *The Doors* (1991). Led Zeppelin used to stay here, in the hedonistic 1970s, as did country-rock legend Gram Parsons and, later, rocker Axl Rose and film director Tim Burton.

The hotel was considerably more rundown when Balazs purchased it for $12 million in 1990. He embarked on a meticulous restoration, aimed at retaining period details and a bohemian spirit while upgrading service and adding contemporary

amenities and polish. Prices have nearly doubled since the renovation and room rates now run from $250 to $1,800 a night.

Chateau guests and nonguests can patronize the adjacent Bar Marmont, a high-style nightspot just on the east flank of the hotel. Opened by Balazs and partner Sean MacPherson in 1995, it's an exotic, erotic getaway that features such mind-bending touches as horsehide walls, butterflies on the ceiling, and a stuffed peacock walking up a mirror. MacPherson, who resides at the Marmont, says it was inspired by a fictional story about a French aristocrat who created a similar hideaway bar in Paris.

The Hyatt House (8401 Sunset), a contemporary 13-story hotel tower across from the Mondrian, was notorious in the 1970s and 1980s as unofficial innkeeper for traveling rock 'n' roll bands. Dubbed the "Riot House," the hotel tolerated wild antics and orgies from bands such as Led Zeppelin, Aerosmith, and Guns N' Roses, merely presenting bills for damages as the guests departed. In the Oscar-winning movie *Almost Famous* (2000), this is the hotel where the fictional band Stillwater and rock groupie Penny Lane (Kate Hudson) party while in L.A.

In 1996, encouraged by the success of

the Mondrian and the House of Blues, the Hyatt sank $3.5 million into a renovation,

Exotic interior of the Bar Marmont. Opposite: The Chateau Marmont's entrance, marked by a series of graceful porticos.

decking out the place in blond wood and stylish black-and-white geometrics. Rather than playing down its raucous past, the hotel paid homage to it during a tour for the press. Staffers dressed up as rockers and groupies to recount tales of

Harley Davidsons driven down hallways and televisions tossed from windows. The hotel still has its heated rooftop swimming pool and, of course, balcony views of the action on the Strip. First built as the Gene Autry Hotel in 1958, it became the Continental Hyatt in 1966.

Another venue key to the comeback of the Strip is the Viper Room (8852 Sunset at Larrabee Street), the live music club opened in 1993 by co-owners Sal Jenco and actor Johnny Depp. The club got a dark burst of notoriety early on, when actor River Phoenix left his life on the sidewalk in front after overdosing on drugs he scored in the club's bathroom. Fans left shrines on the grungy patch of cement, but the club eventually shook off the tragedy and emerged as an essential spot for A&R execs to discover and sign new talent, as well as for fans to catch surprise shows by major bands. Joan Osborne, Pearl Jam, Johnny Cash, and Counting Crows have done unannounced gigs here; the Crows' Adam Duritz sometimes tends bar. The venue was formerly an authentic dive called the Central and, before that, a mobster hangout called the Melody Room.

A weekly dance and choreography showcase distinguishes the Key Club (9039

Cruising Through the Ages

Parking is eight dollars; a cocktail, ten dollars. The high costs of patronizing Sunset Strip bars and nightclubs, not to mention age restrictions, mean that many young people make do with cruising past the excitement rather than paying to participate.

Drinking, blaring music, showing off a hot set of wheels, and calling out to people on the sidewalk have been Strip rituals for generations, accelerating in the 1990s as prices crept up. In response, the West Hollywood sheriff's substation initiated a crackdown on cruising, setting up checkpoints on weekend nights and handing out substantial fines to motorists who passed by more than once in a four-hour period.

Merchants applauded, claiming it cleared the streets for paying patrons; visitors howled that it had become a crime to get lost. Motorists complained that the check- points made traffic tie-ups worse and pointed out that some of the circling around was because it was tough to find parking. Enforcement has waxed and waned with the political currents. For now, the thumping bass beat from hundreds of car stereos—and the battle for control of the Strip—goes on.

town, was world famous in the 1960s as a Sunset Strip pacesetter.

More than just music and dining animates the Strip at night; comedy has long been an important part of the mix. For nearly 30 years the Comedy Store (8433 Sunset) has helped launch such influential talents as Jim Carrey, Robin Williams, Richard Pryor, Andy Kaufman, Sam Kinison, Damon Wayans, Jimmy Walker, Redd Fox, and Arsenio Hall, among many others. Launched in 1972 by owner Mitzi Shore, it was formerly a celebrated nightclub called Ciro's, part of the glamorous history of the Strip in an earlier era.

·····················

Above, left: Electronic enforcement of the Strip's "no cruising" policy. Above, right: Fans leave a shrine to River Phoenix outside the Viper Room. Opposite: The Trocadero, the Strip's original hot spot, in 1938.

Sunset), also a slick, high-tech venue for live performances. The boxy black nightclub called the Roxy (9009 Sunset) has been one of the Strip's most important music venues since 1972. Bruce Springsteen gave a breakthrough concert here in 1975, and countless career-launching shows have since taken place before an audience heavy on music industry types. The Rainbow Bar & Grill next door (9015 Sunset) is a favored rock star hangout, but in the 1950s it was the Villa Nova restaurant, where Joe DiMaggio met Marilyn Monroe on a blind date. The Whisky a Go-Go (8901 Sunset), where acts from Sheryl Crow to X have made their mark on this

Earlier Days on the Strip

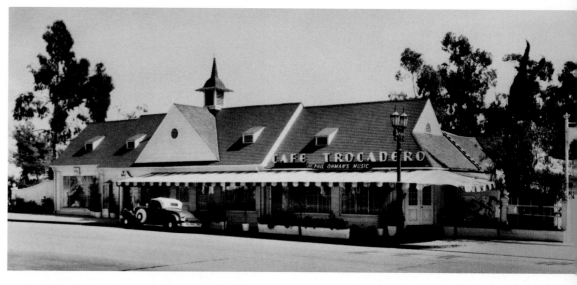

Despite its current allure, the Sunset Strip was decidedly unglamorous well into the 1920s. Hollywood and Beverly Hills thrived, but the path between them was merely a dirt track lined with avocado trees and poinsettia fields. In the rainy season, water cascaded down from the hills, turning the street into a river of mud. The Red Car line from Hollywood was no help—the tracks stopped at the corner of Sunset and Laurel Canyon Boulevard; everything west of there was referred to as "no man's land."

The Strip wasn't even part of Los Angeles. It was unincorporated, part of a township founded in 1896 and named Sherman, after General Moses Sherman, a local mass transit pioneer. In the mid-1920s, as Hollywood's fame spread, merchants succeeded in changing the township's name to West Hollywood, in hopes that a little stardust would rub off and improve their fortunes.

But, starting in 1919, something else was working in the area's favor—Prohibition. Surrounded by orchards, the Strip was considered far enough away from downtown Los Angeles and Hollywood for a lot of things to pass unnoticed. The speakeasies and brothels that sprang up in taverns and private homes were outside the jurisdiction of the Los Angeles police department, and for a time, at least, the county sheriffs went easy on them.

In 1924, the first significant commercial development occurred where today's Sunset Plaza stands. Brothers Francis and George Montgomery constructed four elegant Georgian-style buildings, each containing several shops, in the heart of the Strip. Within a few years construction began nearby on the luxurious towers of the Chateau Marmont and what is today the Argyle. A restaurant and bar, the Russian Eagle, opened in Sunset Plaza and flourished, drawing Rudolph Valentino as a regular, until it mysteriously burned in 1930. In its place a new nightspot, La Boheme, began drawing a crowd, particularly as insiders got word of the gambling operation concealed in its basement.

Meanwhile, entrepreneur and publisher Billy Wilkerson had opened his first restaurant, the Vendome, at 6666 Sunset in Hollywood. Convenient to the offices of Wilkerson's daily entertainment trade paper, *The Hollywood Reporter*, the Vendome saved him the trouble of driving around to call on clients and sources. They could easily be persuaded to turn up at his restaurant, particularly since lunching there made it likely their names would turn up in *The Reporter*.

Wilkerson enjoyed the restaurant business so much that he wanted to expand.

Anticipating the repeal of Prohibition, he purchased a large store of French champagne from a smuggler's boat and stored the bounty in the wine cellar of La Boheme, which had closed. He then bought the whole club, remodeling it after a restaurant he'd seen in Paris. He called it the Trocadero, for the Trocadero Plaza in front of the Eiffel Tower. The elegant nightspot opened at 8610 Sunset in 1934, just as Prohibition laws were lifted.

Opening night was a sensation, attracting such stars as Bing Crosby, Fred Astaire, Jean Harlow, and William Powell, and writer Dorothy Parker. But the following night, the club was empty. Thinking quickly, Wilkerson locked the doors and instructed the band to keep playing. He told the trickle of callers and arrivals that the place was not only sold out but booked solid for two weeks. Word got around, and suddenly "the Troc" was the hottest ticket in town, taking in $3.8 million in its first three years.

The Trocadero thrived for decades, setting the style for a string of glamorous nightspots up and down the Strip. Entertainers like Nat King Cole, or Harl Smith and his Continental Orchestra, performed against painted panoramas of the Parisian skyline. A Sunday night "amateur hour" gave early exposure to Judy Garland, Phil Silvers, and Jackie Gleason. On Saturday nights, the smoke-filled back room hosted a high-stakes poker game in which moguls such as Irving Thalberg, Darryl Zanuck, Carl Laemmle Jr., and Sam Goldwyn wagered their fat profits from the movie industry. Local mobsters including Mickey Cohen, Bugsy Siegel, Tony Cornero, and Wilkerson's good friend Johnny Roselli showed up regularly, as did many of the day's movie stars. The club stood at the eastern fringe of the Sunset Plaza area until it was demolished in 1963. Today, a cocktail bar, the Sunset Trocadero Lounge, pays homage to the original a short distance away at 8280 Sunset.

Wilkerson, however, had sold the place in 1938, and in 1940 opened a new hot spot, Ciro's, at 8433 Sunset, the site of the present-day Comedy Store. The new club had a sleek white exterior that belied its baroque interior, complete with red ceilings, red-silk sofas, and pale green ribbed-silk draperies. For almost 20 years, Ciro's was *the* place. Gable and Lombard, Lucy and Desi, Henry Fonda and Jimmy Stewart, all were regulars, as were Garland, Cary Grant, Katharine Hepburn, and Marlene Dietrich. Gossip columnists Hedda Hopper and Louella Parsons made it their headquarters, perched eagle-eyed by their telephones, watching for benders, brawls, and assignations.

Wilkerson wasn't the only successful nightclub operator on the Strip. Renowned movie writer and director Preston Sturges

....
Preston Sturges Players Club in its 1940s heyday. Opposite: Swanky Ciro's when Nat King Cole headlined.

opened the Players Club in 1940, adjacent to the Chateau Marmont. Actors who patronized the hotel also favored the club, whose name referred to their ancient trade. Garbo, Dietrich, and Hedy Lamarr were among the regulars. The club's Japanese-style building still stands, serving today as a raucous sushi bar called Miyagi's (8225

Sunset). Among the other big "players" were promoters Felix Young and ex-agent Charlie Morrison, who upped the Strip's glamour ante in 1941 when they opened a nightspot called the Mocambo at 8588 Sunset, on the site of the former Versailles club. In a splashy, exotic, Mexican- and Cuban-

The Famous *Players Restaurant* — Hollywood, Cal.

themed setting, the Mocambo featured a dazzling aviary of live birds, including macaws, parakeets, lovebirds, and cockatoos. A $10 cover charge made it an exclusive destination, and the stars flocked in to see and be seen.

In fewer than 20 years, the Sunset Strip had been transformed—from a dirt road in "no man's land" to a teeming thoroughfare and trend-setting nocturnal playground. Its odd, in-between location had become its destiny, as the stars who established homes in Beverly Hills found it a convenient place to dine and drink as they drove through on their way home from the studios. And its unincorporated status appealed to talent agents; they discovered a county loophole that taxed their commissions at a lower rate than in the city of Los Angeles, and moved their offices there.

From 1934 to 1954, the Sunset Strip experienced a night life the likes of which has not been seen again. But by the mid-1950s, club owners were feeling the squeeze as television began keeping people home at night by offering for free, courtesy of Lawrence Welk and Ed Sullivan, some of the same entertainers who played in their clubs. At the same time, another "Strip"—this one 400 miles away in Las Vegas—was luring away marquee entertainers with salaries 10 times as high as they could earn in Los Angeles.

To be sure, the Sunset Strip was hardly dead. It was still the local playground for such "Rat Pack" entertainers as Dean Martin, Sammy Davis Jr., Frank Sinatra, and Jerry Lewis. Comedy clubs such as the Interlude featured the edgy, irreverent talents of Mort Sahl, Lenny Bruce, and Don Rickles, who were introducing a new, politically aware brand of comedy. But popular culture and music were about to change forever with the introduction in 1956 of a sultry-eyed Memphis truck driver named Elvis Presley. Seemingly overnight, the music of "squares" was out, and a rock 'n' roll-fueled youth culture was born.

By 1958, courtesy of television, the Sunset Strip would emerge in the public consciousness as the locale of a hit ABC television show called "77 Sunset Strip," featuring a fictional detective agency run by stars Efrem Zimbalist Jr. and Roger Smith. Their sidekick was Edd "Kookie" Byrnes, a comb-wielding teen who worked as a valet parking attendant. Byrnes became a teen heartthrob—even making a Top 10 record called "Kookie, Kookie, Lend Me Your Comb" that sold two million

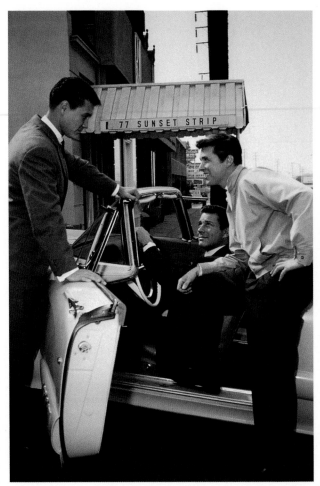

copies. Suddenly, this fabled stretch of asphalt entered the address books of teens and TV watchers across the country.

Action on Sunset Strip picked up again in 1964 with the opening of a club that would become one of the most famous nightspots in the history of rock music. At the corner of Sunset and North Clark Drive, a former Chicago cop with Mob ties named Elmer Valentine launched a discotheque called the Whisky a Go-Go. It was patterned on a club he'd seen in Paris, where patrons had lined up to pay to dance in the crazy, free-form new style.

The Whisky opened with a live act, a young guitar virtuoso named Johnny Rivers who played three sets a night of infectious rock 'n' roll, covering the tunes of Chuck Berry, Bobby Darin, and Ray Charles. In between sets, Valentine had a "girl" disc jockey—unheard of at the time—spinning records from a glass-walled cage high above the dance floor. The first night, the young woman began spontaneously dancing to the music—and the crowd was mesmerized.

It was only because the Whisky was so small that Valentine had suspended the DJ booth in the air. But he quickly realized he was on to something. He installed dancing girls in two more "cages," and a seamstress came up with a look—fringed dresses and short white boots. The "go-go girl" had been born.

The Whisky began to draw sell-out crowds. Regulars in those days included Steve McQueen, Jayne Mansfield, and Cary Grant. Elizabeth Taylor, Warren Beatty, and Jack Nicholson turned up, too. At the time, there was nothing else like the Whisky in America, and the media jumped on the story. *Life* magazine wrote it up. When the Beatles came to Los Angeles on their first American tour, they made a beeline for the Whisky— not to perform but to join in the fun.

Down the Strip, the moribund Ciro's reopened as a rock club. A local band, the Byrds, made it their home base and scored a No. 1 national hit with "Mr. Tambourine Man," an electrified folk version of the Bob Dylan song. By the summer of 1966, the Doors had become the house band at the Whisky.

The mood on the Strip was loosened up fast as the area became a magnet for adventurous kids from throughout the nation. The hair got longer, the clothes wilder, the new social freedom more apparent. Clubs and coffeehouses sprang up to cater to the young—the Sea Witch, the Trip, the London Fog, the Fifth Estate, the Galaxy.

Among the most popular was Pandora's Box, an all-ages hangout precariously situated on a concrete island in the middle of Sunset Boulevard at Crescent Heights. The crowds got so thick at Pandora's Box that the kids spilled into the street, causing endless traffic tie-ups. Merchants complained, and the police came out in force to "hassle" the young folk to keep them moving along.

In November of 1966, county officials decided Pandora's Box should be demolished and its island eliminated to improve traffic flow. In the charged atmosphere of the times, the kids took it personally, and thousands showed up to demonstrate on the night of November 13. They held hands, played guitar, and shouted, "Give us back our Strip!" Traffic backed up and the cops cracked down. A bus was overturned and a riot broke out. In the end, 300 arrests were made and the melee, now known as the "Riot on the Sunset Strip," made front-page news. Among the crowd on the scene that night were Sonny and Cher, Dennis Hopper and Peter Fonda, Bob Denver of *Gilligan's Island*, and Stephen Stills.

Stills, a Texas-born songwriter and musician, already owed a karmic debt to Sunset Boulevard. Idling in a Sunset Strip traffic jam several years earlier, he'd looked over and spotted his old pal Neil Young driving a 1953 hearse. Young was just down from Canada to seek his musical fortune. He and Stills hooked up to form the influential Buffalo Springfield, which briefly became the house band at the Whisky.

Observing the riot on the Strip that night, Stills heard guitar chords chiming in his head and was inspired to write "For What's It's Worth (Stop, Hey, What's That Sound)." The spookily accurate tune became the unofficial wakeup call for a generation, an anthem that would become associated with more significant events, including the riots at the 1968 Democratic Convention and the war in Vietnam, and go on to put Buffalo Springfield on the map.

Stills and Young would segue into a different group—Crosby, Stills, Nash and Young—that would become hugely successful and influential.

Pandora's Box was eventually bulldozed and the traffic island removed. But that hardly quelled the youth movement. The flower-power parade along the Strip's narrow sidewalks swelled through the summer of 1967, becoming a full-fledged carnival and, at times, a freak show for incredulous adults and gawking out-of-towners. In the end, though, it was this generation and its rock music that created a whole new business for the Strip, saving it from the moribund destiny that enveloped Hollywood once the studios moved out.

Until the 1960s, the recording industry had been an endeavor of fairly modest profits, based mostly in New York. But rock 'n' roll was transforming the business, and hungry producers were on the lookout for the next big acts. In the 1960s, the Strip was brimming with new talent. A four-part harmony group called the Mamas and the Papas, led by John Phillips, had struggled in Greenwich Village but scored a record deal within a month of moving to L.A. In less than a year, the group had two hit singles, "California Dreaming" and "Monday, Monday." The Turtles, Sonny and Cher, Arthur Lee and Love, Frank Zappa, Joni Mitchell, the Byrds, the Doors—all were fixtures at clubs on the Strip.

In the summer of 1966, the Doors grad-

Opposite: "Sunset pigs," as described in Joni Mitchell's song "California," advance to quell youthful riots on the Strip in 1966. Billboards behind them promote a competing scene.

uated from the divey London Fog to the Whisky next door, debuting songs like "Light My Fire," "Break On Through," and "The End." Crowds at first rejected front man Jim Morrison's dark intensity, then embraced it. But when the Dionysian lead singer went overboard one night, improvising Oedipal lyrics to "The End" that shocked the club's management, the Doors were fired before ever releasing an album. They never played the Whisky again. It scarcely mattered. The group signed with Elektra Records, and the label bought the band members the first Sunset Strip billboard ever devoted to a record album. Their faces, larger than life, haunted the Strip in the summer of 1967 under the words "The Doors Break On Through With an Electrifying Album."

Besides announcing a group that was destined to break big, the billboard heralded a new order on the Strip. Suddenly, record executives were the ones driving the flashy cars, occupying the plush office towers, and keeping the toniest restaurants in business. Outsized billboards became mandatory for every major record release; the only thing negotiable was how long they would stay up.

Throughout the decade, the West Coast record business had been growing. First Capitol Records emerged; then in 1961, Liberty Records set up shop at 6920 Sunset and went on to release hits by Jan and Dean, the Hollies, and the Spencer Davis Group, before evolving into United Artists and then EMI. Herb Alpert and Jerry Moss formed A&M Records in 1966, with offices at Charlie Chaplin's former studios on La Brea, and were instantly successful. Motown Records moved to Hollywood from Detroit in 1970, joining labels like Polydor and Elektra. Talent manager and deal maker David Geffen emerged as a mover and shaker in the late 1960s, opening an office with partner Elliot Roberts at 9130 Sunset and forming the Asylum record label. Its roster of singer-songwriters, including Joni Mitchell, Jackson Browne, Linda Ronstadt, and the Eagles, came to define the so-called "California sound" of the 1970s.

The magnetic power of the Strip somehow drew the right combination of people in the late 1960s and early 1970s, translating the music of the street kids into plush corporate offices up and down the boulevard. As a result, a profitable industry was established and the Sunset Strip had a lasting new lease on life.

The Dark Side of the Strip

More than any other stretch of Sunset Boulevard, the Strip has been a magnet for corruption and vice. The outlandish cash generated by entertainment industry profits and real estate bonanzas meant there were appetites to be sated and the money to pay for it. Every known stripe of mobster, hustler, promoter, and panderer has stepped up to get a piece of the action at one time or another.

In the 1920s and 1930s, brothels, speakeasies, and gambling joints flourished in homes in the hills above the Strip. One—the Colony, a speak-easy on Alta Loma Road above Sunset—drew gambling crowds that the sheriff's department conveniently ignored. Another, the Clover Club, was a fortress for high rollers located just above Sunset at La Cienega. Its wealthy patrons brought so much cash with them that they were sometimes met at their cars by machine gun-toting casino employees, who escorted them to the gambling tables for their own protection. Some customers would drop thousands—even hundreds of thousands—in an evening.

The elegant salons of the Clover Club were run by Guy McAfee, whose years as a vice squad officer had made him wise to tricks that might foil the authorities. McAfee had the club install secret panels, one-way mirrors, and an extra-long driveway. When officials arrived, casino operators had an extra 45 seconds to hide the illegal loot, flip over the gaming tables, and transform the salon into a harmless-looking tea parlor. The ruse even worked a few times. But the place was too flashy to be ignored, and law enforcement was relentless. One raid, conducted with 300 celebrities in the place, netted $15,000 worth of gambling equipment, including six roulette wheels. The Clover Club was gone by 1938, in the wake of grand jury investigations and the recall of Mayor Frank Shaw.

A few gay clubs and drag shows operated on the hush-hush at places like Johnny's Backyard on Ivar Avenue, or the Barn on Cahuenga Boulevard, just south of Sunset. The authorities raided them at will. At least one gay gathering spot seemed to operate with impunity—the elegant Cafe Gala, a supper club above Sunset, where movieland sophisticates could "be themselves" while listening to Cole Porter tunes played on dueling grand pianos.

As ever, there were brothels. A series of madams catered to the better-paying Hollywood trade in the 1920s and 1930s, finding creative ways to smooth it over with the cops. One was Lee Francis, who operated a brothel in the 1930s at the Piazza del Sol, at 8349 Sunset, just west of the present-day Comedy Store. (The Spanish Revival structure, preserved as a historic landmark, now houses film production offices.) When the vice squad showed at the "House of Francis," as it was called, she hid her girls and greeted the officers with champagne on ice and Russian caviar. When Francis' luck ran out, her place was taken by Ann Forrester, the so-called "Black Widow," who raked in $5,000 a week in the late 1930s and kept customers' names on file for leverage. But the vice squad closed her down, too.

Into the gap stepped Brenda Allen, a red-headed looker who took the business, along with the notion of protection, to new levels. Allen rented a series of ornate party houses above the Strip, moving on to the next one after each of her 19 arrests. At her peak, in the 1940s, she had 114 young women taking in $9,000 a day from johns who paid $20 to $100 for their favors. Allen took 50% off the top. Later, she testified

....

Gangster Mickey Cohen, the self-styled "King of the Sunset Strip," displays the compulsion that saved his life on at least one occasion. Opposite: Cops check up on vice outside a burlesque club in 1956.

that she spent a third of her income paying off cops, doctors, lawyers, and bail bondsmen. Part of the fix went to her boyfriend, a badge-wearing LAPD vice sergeant, Elmer V. Jackson, whom she cut in for profits as well as personal favors. Their alliance was eventually uncovered, spurring a grand jury

investigation. Allen took as many down with her as she could, including Police Chief Clemence B. Horrall, who was forced into early retirement.

Like nearly every nightclub mecca, the Strip drew money and interference from the Mob. In the mid-1940s, when Benjamin "Bugsy" Siegel turned his focus toward Las Vegas, he left his L.A. gambling interests in the hands of a lieutenant named Mickey Cohen. The real-life gangster described in the movie and novel L.A. Confidential, Cohen had grown up poor in Los Angeles' Jewish enclave of Boyle Heights, one of six children raised by a widowed mother. From back-alley craps, the young Cohen graduated to boxing, bootlegging, and racketeering. Only five-foot-five, and nothing much to look at, Cohen craved attention and got it by dressing in flashy suits and snap-brim fedoras, and by tipping lavishly. Once on top, Cohen made a habit of chumming around with reporters and gossip columnists, who relished the connection because stories about Cohen helped sell newspapers.

At the height of his fame, Cohen kept a haberdashery on Sunset Boulevard. A front for bookmaking, it carried suits and hats—but only in his size. By 1947, Cohen was raking in an estimated $80,000 a month from gambling, bookmaking, and loan sharking and had become known as "the King of the Sunset Strip."

A rival gangster, Jack Dragna, tried to muscle in, setting off a series of violent incidents known as the "Sunset Wars." One day in 1948, three gunmen, including Jimmy "The Weasel" Frattiano, walked into Cohen's haberdashery and started blasting away. The bullets killed his bodyguard, but Cohen survived because he had stepped into the bathroom. As it happened, Cohen was a clean freak who washed his hands 50 times a day. That day, the quirk saved his life. That same year, Dragna's men made another attempt on Cohen's life, rigging dynamite to go off at his Brentwood home. The blast left a crater 20 feet wide where Cohen's bed had been—but the gangster wasn't in it, and he survived. A year later, Cohen was out for a late dinner at Sherry's restaurant, at 8106 Sunset near Crescent Heights. As he emerged with a party of oth-

ers, gunmen hiding beneath a billboard across the street unleashed a hail of bullets. Again, a bodyguard was killed. Cohen took a bullet but survived.

The "Sunset Wars" dragged on for a year, until Chicago mobster Sam Giancana stepped in to negotiate a truce. By then the Feds were looking into Cohen's taxes and had discovered he wasn't paying any. He went to prison for four years. Upon release, he got back to busi-

Top: Gunmen hiding under the billboard at left fired across the street at Cohen, who survived. Bottom photo, also from 1949, shows Sherry's, the target, from the shooter's vantage behind the billboard.

ness, "milking" the Strip by sending a hatbox around to club owners with instructions that it be filled with cash and returned to his haberdashery.

But the action on the Strip was drying up. And so was Cohen's luck. In 1962 he was convicted again of income tax evasion and sent to prison for 15 years. While there, he was attacked and left partially paralyzed by a fellow inmate wielding a lead pipe. He returned to the Strip upon his release in 1976 but, broke and powerless, he didn't get much started. He died that year of stomach cancer. Ⓢ

Check it out: The Sunset Strip

Food and Drink

Asia de Cuba, 8440 Sunset Boulevard, (323) 848-6000. Upscale, trendy hot spot in Mondrian Hotel. Imaginative cuisine fuses Asian, Cuban elements. Inside tables loud, lively; patio dining offers magical city views.

Barfly, 8730 Sunset Boulevard, (310) 360-9490. Svelte spinoff of Paris watering hole, favored by models, actors, agents, music biz hustlers. Restaurant, full bar.

Cajun Bistro, 8301 Sunset Boulevard, (323) 656-6388. New Orleans-style seafood grill. Formerly the Source health food restaurant, sent up in *Annie Hall*.

Joss, 9255 Sunset Boulevard, (310) 276-1886. Acclaimed *haute* Chinese cuisine. Full bar, wine list.

Le Dome, 8720 Sunset Boulevard, (310) 659-6919. Classic French continental cuisine, old-school celebrity watching.

Fenix, 8358 Sunset Boulevard (at Argyle Hotel), (323) 848-6677. First-rate California-French cuisine, Deco-fabulous surroundings, city views.

Mirabelle, 8768 Sunset Boulevard, (310) 659-6022. A mainstay for food, drinks, Strip-watching since the early 1970s.

Bar Marmont, 8171 Sunset Boulevard, (323) 650-0575. Exotic, velvet-rope bar adjacent to Chateau Marmont.

Skybar, 8440 Sunset Boulevard, (323) 650-8999. Dreamy poolside cocktail environment with dramatic city views. Abuts Mondrian Hotel; admission guaranteed to hotel guests.

The Coffee House, 8226 Sunset Boulevard, (323) 848-7007. Stylish, spacious, comfortable hang offering sandwiches, soup. Adjacent newsstand.

Mel's Drive-In, 8585 Sunset Boulevard, (310) 854-7200. Quality diner food, retro '50s decor in spin-off of California spot that inspired *American Graffiti*. Formerly Ben Frank's, a longtime Strip landmark and musician's hangout.

Duke's Tropicana Coffee Shop, 8909 Sunset Boulevard, (310) 652-3100. Hole-in-the wall diner adjacent to Whisky favored by long-haired rockers and slumming movie stars.

Live Music and Comedy Venues

House of Blues, 8430 Sunset Boulevard, (323) 848-5100. Top rock, pop, blues bookings in "Delta roadhouse" filled with outsider art. Restaurant, bar, weekend gospel brunch.

Comedy Store, 8433 Sunset Boulevard, (323) 656-6225. Strip's top comedy showcase since early 1970s. Helped launch Robin Williams, Jim Carrey, Andy Kaufman, and Richard Pryor, among others.

Key Club, 9039 Sunset Boulevard, (310) 786-1712. Live music, disco, monthly choreography showcase nights.

Roxy, 9009 Sunset Boulevard, (310) 278-9457. Longtime record industry showcase for emerging and established rock, pop acts.

Rainbow Bar & Grill, 9015 Sunset Boulevard, (310) 278-4232. Restaurant, bar favored by rockers, music biz.

Viper Room, 8852 Sunset Boulevard, (310) 358-1880. Essential Strip venue for rock and roll.

Whisky a Go-Go, 8901 Sunset Boulevard, (310) 652-4202. Historic disco and live music showcase.

Specialty Shopping

Tower Records, 8801 Sunset Boulevard, (310) 657-7300. Chain's flagship store, famed for wide selection, in-store signings, performances. Classical, video outlets across the street.

Book Soup, 8818 Sunset Boulevard, (310) 659-3110. Strip's mainstay literary hub, frequent in-store signings. Literature, art, and travel books, newsstand.

Tracey Ross, 8595 Sunset Boulevard, (310) 854-1996. Intimate boutique featuring casual clothing, jewelry. Caters to models, actors, rich kids. Part of Sunset Plaza collection of high-end shops, sidewalk cafes.

Beverly Hills

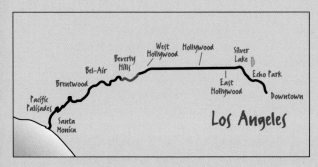

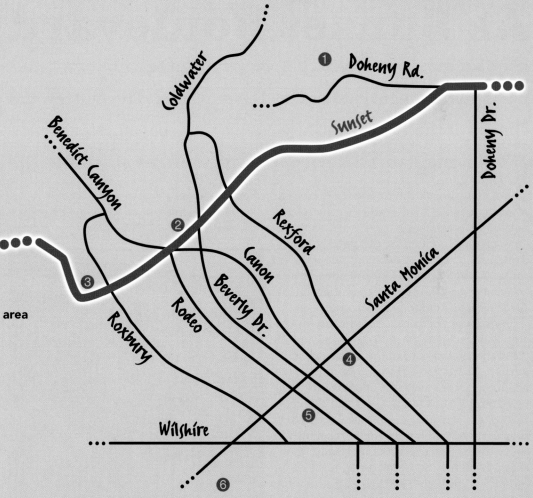

1 **Greystone Mansion**

2 **Beverly Hills Hotel**

3 **Dead Man's Curve**

4 **Beverly Hills City Hall**

5 **Prime Rodeo Drive shopping area**

6 **Beverly Hills High School**

The Beverly Hills Hotel, circa 1920.

As Sunset Boulevard

heads west, past Doheny Drive, a dramatic change takes place the moment one enters Beverly Hills. The clutter and energy of the Strip vanish, yielding to a soothing landscape of lush, manicured lawns and high hedges shielding the

fabled mansions of the rich and celebrated. A grassy center divider adds to the neighborhood's patrician, leisurely atmosphere. Originally used as a bridle path for residents and their horses to clip-clop gaily en route to house parties and picnics, it was converted to a landscaped median in the 1940s when automobile traffic increased.

Long the "bedroom community of the stars," Beverly Hills is linked indelibly in the public mind with luxury and excess, with Judith Krantz novels and Rodeo Drive shopping sprees, face lifts and psychotherapy, "Beverly Hills 90210" and "The Beverly Hillbillies." Its glitzy commercial district, the so-called Golden Triangle, lies south of Sunset near the intersection of Santa Monica and Wilshire boulevards and justifies its name with a jewelry store and a beauty

shop on virtually every corner. The city—5.7 square miles and about 33,000 residents, all of them completely surrounded by the city

of Los Angeles—has, according to one recent count, 129 banks and financial institutions, 124 securities firms and brokerages, and 336 real estate companies.

The area around Sunset Boulevard is strictly residential, save for the historic Beverly Hills Hotel. It's one of the posher areas in a famously posh city—nearly every house is a showplace, and the median annual household income exceeds $250,000. Along wide, curving side streets lined with dizzying palms lies a treasure trove of addresses of stars and former stars that for decades have drawn tour buses and looky-loos.

Ironically, for a symbol of the good life, Beverly Hills was born because of a business plan that failed. Speculators had purchased the land in the early days of the 20th century to drill for oil, but wells repeatedly came up dry. What the drilling did divine, however, was water, a scarce and valuable commodity in the days before the Los Angeles aqueduct was constructed.

· ·

The grassy median strip along Sunset Boulevard is all that is left of the bridle path that was a principal transportation lane in early Beverly Hills. Opposite: An aerial view of expansive, lushly landscaped homes shows exactly why Beverly Hills is synonymous with luxurious living.

Capitalizing on the discovery, the Rodeo Land and Water Company was formed in 1906 under president Burton Green, who decided to build a residential community. Green realized that the trick would be attracting the proper kind of customer— one with enough money and leisure to view the development's 11-mile distance from downtown as an asset rather than as a hindrance.

Green envisioned a prestigious residential enclave with the finest amenities, such as wide, curving boulevards; spacious lots with generous setbacks; and abundant parks and trees. He hired top architects, engineers, and landscape designers to lay the groundwork. So many trees were planted that even today, it is estimated Beverly Hills has one public tree for every resident. Green built himself a splendid Tudor mansion with a swimming pool, and named the town Beverly, after his former home in Beverly Farms, Massachusetts. The name was soon amended to Beverly Hills to capitalize on the slopes north of Sunset.

For several years, it appeared the development scheme would go bust—one more failed dream among the fields of lima beans that seemed to be the only thing thriving. By 1910, only six permanent

homes had been established. Then the persistent Green and his company tried a tactic that had worked for the railroad companies—building a luxury hotel in the middle of nowhere, at which prospective land buyers could be seduced into sharing the developers' vision.

The opulent Beverly Hills Hotel began to rise like a splendid mirage against its bleak surroundings. Built in the Spanish Mission style for what was then a whopping $500,000, it was lushly landscaped and featured a splendid swimming pool. (The structure was originally painted white; the famous pink paint, along with other significant design elements, weren't introduced until 1948.) The hotel opened May 1, 1912, to great fanfare, with invitations billing it as "halfway between Los Angeles and the sea." Margaret Anderson, who had established high standards for dealing with the rich at the Hollywood Hotel, was lured to manage the place and she made a great success of it.

That same year, something else happened that would pave the way for the future of Beverly Hills—movie star Douglas Fairbanks decided to build a home there for himself and his lady love, "America's Sweetheart" Mary Pickford.

No matter that each of them was still married to another. Fairbanks boldly filed for divorce, and proceeded to turn a rough hunting lodge in the hills above the new hotel into a mansion. Pickford soon filed divorce papers of her own, and the two were married at their new estate, which the press dubbed Pickfair.

The pair moved in and began to entertain lavishly. Their presence did wonders for real estate values. "The house Doug built for Mary" became the center of Beverly Hills social life—playing host to not just movie people, but visiting royalty and diverse celebrities such as Albert Einstein and Charles Lindbergh. Suddenly, all the top movie stars were in a rush to live in Beverly Hills. In the Roaring '20s, with income tax still unheard of and the movies unchallenged as America's favorite form of entertainment, the stars had absurd amounts of money to lavish on their estates.

Among the first to build houses in the new celebrity enclave were Rudolph Valentino, Charlie Chaplin, Gloria Swanson, Buster Keaton, John Barrymore, Pola Negri, Tom Mix, and Harold Lloyd. Lloyd, who'd reaped full value for his silent comedies by starting his own production outfit, spent $2 million on his paradisiacal Green Acres, a 44-room mansion on 16 superbly landscaped acres that included a lake, a forest, stables, a boathouse, and spectacular fountains. In 1922 Thomas Ince, a prolific producer of Westerns, set the style for Beverly Hills movie tycoons with the estate he called *Dias Dorados* (Golden Days). The mansion ran more than 300 feet in length, from the grand party room at one end to the summer kitchen at the other.

Studios moguls like Sam Goldwyn, Harry Cohn, and David O. Selznick hurried to build Beverly Hills showplaces of their own. A fabled and festive lifestyle developed, filled with tennis, horseback riding, and weekend polo matches, plus big automobiles and grand catered parties—and the social secretaries to arrange everything. Never mind that only a decade before, entrenched society had viewed movie people as rogues and fly-by-nighters. Wealth begat respectability in a frontier town like early Los Angeles.

People with fortunes from oil, banking, and manufacturing began to join the migration. Edward L. Doheny, whose oil strike had launched the turn-of-the-century petroleum boom in Los Angeles, spent $4 million to build his 55-room Greystone Mansion, then a 410-acre ranch with riding stables, tennis courts, and a separate seven-room cottage for the grandchildren. It was completed in 1927. Will Rogers, the beloved humorist, built a house and began datelining his news-

Will Rogers, who datelined his columns "Beverly Hills," was proclaimed its mayor in 1926 and served one year. Opposite: From its inception, the Beverly Hills Hotel used stylized and evocative brochures to lure wealthy visitors—and potential land buyers.

paper columns "Beverly Hills," which greatly increased the little burg's fame.

In 1926, Rogers was surprised at the train station by a crowd of Beverly Hills friends and neighbors as he returned from a European tour. By motorcade, they carried him to a park across from the Beverly Hills Hotel, where, in a boisterous ceremony, they named him the town's first mayor. Rogers accepted a flower-covered key to the city. "It is my intention to elevate motion picture folk and real estate men to the level of the common people," he quipped. He would later say that his most important duty as mayor was "directing folks to Mary Pickford's house." Rogers' reign was brief, as the California legislature decreed the following year that the mayor be chosen from the city council. But the national press ran with the story, and the image of Beverly Hills as a one-of-a-kind place run by wealthy and fun-loving movie folk took hold in the public imagination.

In the 1930s, Beverly Hills began to develop its Golden Triangle business district, a 20-block section bounded by Wilshire Boulevard, Santa Monica Boulevard, and Rexford Drive. Banks, hotels, and office buildings sprang up, along with the finest retail stores, beauty shops, and four-star restaurants. Industry was discouraged by way of strict planning and zoning regulations. Even today, Beverly Hills' largest employer is the city itself, followed by luxury hotels (including the Regent Beverly Wilshire, Peninsula, and Beverly Hilton), huge talent agencies, high-end department stores, financial brokerages, car dealerships, and banks.

In the 1980s, the long-prized small-town feel gave way to an increasingly international atmosphere as a high number of foreign-born citizens moved in. Many were Iranian Jews who had fled their country after the fall of the shah. Among them were wealthy professionals,

doctors, and lawyers who established practices in Beverly Hills. Others specialized in retail and jewelry, and helped establish the ultra-chic Rodeo Drive shopping area.

Today, despite the changes, Beverly Hills remains the ultra-exclusive residential community that Burton Green envisioned. No longer the "in" place for stars to settle—younger Hollywood prefers Malibu and the Hollywood Hills—it still has so many famous and influential residents that the police department has a ban on "fixing" tickets, as there are just too many people with pull. (Slapping a cop won't go over well either—Zsa Zsa Gabor went to jail for that.)

The population is nearly 90 percent white. The school district is renowned; standardized test scores vastly exceed regional and state averages, and 94 percent of high school graduates go on to college. Beverly Hills does have some residents of modest means, mostly elderly people in rent-controlled apartments south of Santa Monica Boulevard. Surprisingly, the city as a whole has more renters than homeowners, and more Democrats than Republicans.

And of course, if money could buy happiness, Beverly Hills wouldn't have so many therapists, drug abuse counselors, and divorce lawyers. Still, some people claim they couldn't bear to live anywhere else.

Perhaps the most eye-catching building in Beverly Hills is the five-story City Hall tower (455 North Rexford Drive), an ornate and colorful Spanish Baroque design completed in 1932 to reflect the young city's opulent self-image. It stood in for the Beverly Hills police station in the Eddie Mur-

phy movie *Beverly Hills Cop* (1984).

A scant few blocks away is legendary Rodeo Drive, where status-hounds and those who get an erotic charge from overspending can indulge themselves in world-class style. The *crème de la crème* of designers, jewelers, and shoe artisans are all here in the three blocks of Rodeo between Wilshire and Santa Monica boulevards, including Giorgio, Gucci, Hermes, Vuitton, Prada, Bijan, Chanel, Armani, Valentino, Christian Dior, Ralph Lauren, and more.

The lure of this shopping locale started in 1934, when custom tailor Eddie Schmidt opened a men's shop at 300 Rodeo Drive and began selling $150 suits to the likes of Fred Astaire, Tyrone Power, and Robert Taylor. Saks Fifth Avenue opened nearby on Wilshire Boulevard in 1938, joined later by Neiman Marcus (still legendary for its end-of-season sales) and most recently by the extremely popular Barneys New York.

Since 1990, tourists have been flocking to the ersatz European charm of the Spanish Steps leading up off Wilshire to Two Rodeo, a lavish collection of exclusive shops, including Tiffany, Cartier, Sulka, and Charles Jourdan. The cobblestone Via Rodeo walkway that runs through the area was the city's first paved street, dating back to 1914. Nearby on Wilshire is the mammoth Niketown emporium devoted to status athletic gear. Most of the town's major talent agencies are also nearby, as are fine restaurants and the historic Regent Beverly Wilshire Hotel (9500 Wilshire Boulevard), where seasoned shoppers enjoy winding down with afternoon tea.

Above: A couple kiss after marrying in a chapel inside the Rodeo Collection mall. Right: Via Rodeo Drive exudes the feel of a luxurious, if faux, Mediterranean marketplace. Opposite: Rodeo Drive is home to virtually every big name in the retail world.

THE BEVERLY HILLS HOTEL ·
ELMER GREY - ARCHITECT
LOS ANGELES CAL.
MRS. MARGARET J. ANDERSON
STANLEY S. ANDERSON

Five-Star Fun

It's pink, retro, swank, and fabulous—everything it ought to be as the hotel playground to the stars situated directly on Sunset Boulevard in the heart of Beverly Hills. Remodeled in the 1990s for $100 million and reopened in 1995, the five-star Beverly Hills Hotel caters to the show business crowd as well as to certain international visitors and corporate travelers—the kind who can afford nightly room rates that start at $335 and go up to $3,000, give or take a little.

For the entertainment industry, the hotel's Polo Lounge, private bungalows, and poolside cabanas are the place for strutting, preening, profile-raising—and deal-making, particularly at peak occupancy times such as during the Oscar and Grammy ceremonies. Plenty of nonguests make use of the hotel, too—for a casual counter lunch at the Fountain Coffee Shop, with its banana-leaf wallpaper, for a drink at the bar, or for tea and cakes in the lobby piano lounge.

Built amid barren bean fields in 1912, the Mission-style hotel with its red-tile roof was originally part of a campaign to lure prospective home buyers to the area. (The lush park across the street was originally part of the hotel grounds, created to persuade newcomers arriving by trolley that there was something in Beverly Hills.) After opening, the hotel was an immediate hit with society and movie people alike. The restaurant-lounge, originally named *El Jardin*, was where such legendary tipplers as Errol Flynn, W.C. Fields, and John Barrymore chose to hold court, and for a time, its Table One was permanently reserved for Charlie Chaplin.

After the stock market crash in 1929, the hotel closed for three years. It reopened in 1932, operated by Bank of America vice president Hernando Courtright, a Spanish-born *bon vivant* who took to the Hollywood crowd. He installed himself as manager and dedicated himself to the revival. The hotel thrived, exceeding even its former fame. Movie star high jinks became the norm in

....

A rendering of the Beverly Hills Hotel drawn by its architect, Elmer Grey, at about the time of the hotel's opening in 1912. Opposite: The sign outside the hotel is written in its signature script and surrounded by swaying palms and profusely flowering plants.

the 1930s. Clark Gable and Carole Lombard, before they were married, carried on their affair in a bungalow. Katharine Hepburn once dove fully clothed into the pool after a tennis match. Greta Garbo moved in for months, seeking seclusion and taking all her meals in her bungalow. Howard Hughes rented four bungalows at a time, remaining a resident on and off for 30 years.

In 1941, Courtright bought the hotel in partnership with mogul Harry Warner and stars Loretta Young and Irene Dunne. He changed the name of the bar and restaurant to the Polo Lounge, inspired by the sporting escapades of his friend Charlie Wrightsman, who donated for permanent display the silver trophy won by his championship polo team. Horseback hockey was then the rage among stars and movie moguls, and players like Will Rogers, Daryl Zanuck, and Spencer Tracy began gathering at the Polo Lounge after weekend matches at Roger's Pacific Palisades ranch.

The hotel, originally painted white, acquired its famous pink and green colors and tropical motif in 1948, after a significant remodeling by architect Paul Williams. Williams, an African American who designed many signature homes and buildings in Los Angeles during that peri-

od, added the much-photographed Crescent Wing—the flat pink facade bearing the hotel's name in stylized cursive—as well as the Fountain Coffee Shop and many design elements within the lobbies, ballrooms, and staircases.

In the 1950s and 1960s, the celebrity focus shifted to the pool and cabana area, then called the Sand and Surf Club and featuring a sand beach, 21 private cabanas, and swimming lessons by blond Adonis and pool manager Svend Petersen. Physiques could be displayed—and profiles raised—by prearranging well-timed telephone pages. Faye Dunaway learned to swim for a movie role here, and the Beatles once took over the largest cabana for a weekend. The sand is gone, but Petersen endures, along with poolside amenities such as chilled towels and fresh sorbet. In 1978, Neil Simon's hit movie *California Suite*, starring Jane Fonda, Alan Alda, Bill Cosby, and Richard Pryor, was filmed at the hotel and its pool area.

In 1986 the hotel was purchased by oilman Marvin Davis, who sold it the following year, for $50 million more, to the sultan of Brunei, one of the world's richest men by virtue of vast oil deposits in his tiny southeast Asian country. (Staff members claim the new owner, Hassanal Bolkiah, has never been seen on the premises and operates the hotel through a subsidiary that also owns London's Dorchester Hotel). In December 1992, the hotel closed for a two-year renovation that sent many agents, Realtors and deal-makers into a tailspin as they were forced to find a meeting spot other than the Polo Lounge.

Since reopening, it has earned a Mobil five-star rating and moved smoothly back into the center of the area's social scene, hosting countless large-scale charity events in the remodeled ballrooms and gardens. The lobby features a new Tea Lounge, with a gold-leaf-colored Steinway piano decorated with hand-painted birds. Amenities in each of its 203 rooms include three telephones, a plain-paper fax machine, butler service button, and Ralph Lauren linens. The hotel also offers complimentary limousine service for such outings as Beverly Hills shopping excursions.

The Polo Lounge still features slim white telephones beside some of the indoor tables. "There's not as much call for them now that everyone has a cell phone," said publicity director Diana Daniele. "But if someone wants to be paged, we can still arrange it."

Seeing Stars

The stars are often long since dead—or at the very least, away on location—and the houses are usually hidden behind high walls and hedges, but it doesn't seem to matter much. Every year, fans and visitors still buy roughly 100,000 "star maps," many from curbside hawkers along Sunset Boulevard.

Such maps have been a staple of the Los Angeles tourist trade since the 1920s and 1930s, when actors were happy to publicize their homes as part of the glamorous image they cultivated. Picture postcards were even created to tantalize the public with the celebrities' stylish abodes.

The first known guide, created in May 1924 by Don Belding, a disabled war veteran working for the Lord & Thomas advertising agency, listed addresses and specific directions to the homes of 65 prominent screen stars. By the 1930s, home addresses of the stars were routinely included in official publications of the tourist bureau. Illustrated maps soon followed, focusing on Hollywood, Beverly Hills, and Bel-Air. The addresses were usually accurate, culled from real estate records, news clippings, tips from delivery people, and door-to-door sleuthing. But updating the maps rarely seemed to be in the map-sellers' best interests.

Nevertheless, fans kept buying them, encouraged by movie magazine blurbs about stars waving as they emerged in their bathrobes to pick up the morning newspaper. Names like Jimmy Stewart, Doris Day, Lucille Ball, and Milton Berle were on the maps back then, and they still are, mixed with newer but sometimes unreliable listings.

Sightseers are warned not to trespass or ring doorbells—unlikely endeavors in any event, since they will usually encounter gates that block all but the merest glimpses of the abodes. But even a snapshot of an address on a curb or gatepost becomes a magical curio for the devoted fan, who can go away happy to have tread in the vicinity of a charmed dwelling place.

The following is a brief guide to famous homes on or near Sunset Boulevard.

GREYSTONE MANSION (501 North Doheny Road, near the corner of Loma Vista Drive). Just above Sunset on the street named for the oil baron who built it is one of the grandest houses in town, the 55-room Greystone Mansion. With its grounds open to the public ever since it was purchased by the city of Beverly Hills, the mansion offers a glimpse of how the city's ultra rich lived before the stock market crash of

family from violence. In 1929, a disgruntled household employee named Hugh Plunkett shot and killed Edward Doheny Jr., the rich young heir, then turned the gun on himself. Because both corpses were found nude in Doheny's bedroom, many held the murder to be a crime of passion.

The estate passed into the hands of developer Paul Trousdale, who carved the grounds into the subdivision that bears his name, then sold the house to the city of Beverly Hills in 1964. Hollywood came calling, and used the mansion as a location for such movies as *The Witches of Eastwick*, *Batman and Robin*, *Greystoke: The Legend of Tarzan*, *The Loved One*, *Ghostbusters II*, *Indecent Proposal* and *Clueless*, as well as such television shows as *Dynasty* and *Falcon Crest*. From 1969 to 1982, Greystone served as the campus of the American Film Institute. Currently, the property is used for weddings, parties, photo and location shoots, and chamber music concerts.

For dates and times the grounds are open for public touring, call (310) 550-4796.

FORMER MENENDEZ HOUSE (722 Elm Drive, south of Sunset). On a night in August 1989, the privileged sons of Jose and Kitty Menendez, a millionaire entertainment executive and his wife, killed their

1929. Merely a glimpse, though—since its doors are locked and the public is confined to peeking into the windows.

An imposing Tudor of gray limestone

A portrait of Edward Doheny, who built the 55-room Greystone for his son, dominates one wall of the mansion's reception room.

with a slate roof and undulating chimneys, the 46,000-square-foot house was built for $4 million in 1927 and presented as a gift from Edward Doheny to his only son. At the time, the property encompassed 415 acres, making it the largest family estate in Los Angeles.

Wealth, however, couldn't insulate the

Home of Bud Abbott—Home of Lou Costello

Residence of Dorothy Lamour

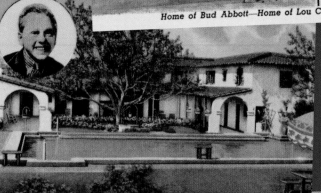
Home of Mickey Rooney

These charming collector cards from the early 1940s (shown actual size) are among the memorabilia created to cash in on the public's interest in the stars and their homes.

Residence of Judy Garland

Home of Shirley Temple

Home of Gene Autry

THALBERG AND SHEARER MANSION
(9419 Sunset, north side). This palatial
stone mansion—built in 1918 by silent film
actress Pauline Fredericks—can just barely
be glimpsed behind high hedges and gates.
In the 1920s, it was the home of boy wonder
MGM movie executive Irving Thalberg, who
married actress Norma Shearer in the backyard in 1927.

**FORMER SITE OF SHEIK AL FASSI MAN-
SION** (9561 Sunset, north side, at Alpine
Drive). Currently a grassy vacant lot, this
site has a colorful history. In the 1830s and
1840s, it contained the adobe ranch house
of the original owner of Beverly Hills, Maria
Rita Valdez de Villa, who had received a
Spanish grant deeding her 4,500 acres, then
called *Rodeo de las Aquas*, on which she
raised cattle and horses.

The name meant "Gathering of the
Waters," describing the rainy season, when
runoff poured down from surrounding
canyons like Coldwater and Benedict to
gather in *cienegas*, or swamps. The area was
then rural and lawless. After surviving a har-
rowing Indian attack in 1852, Valdez made a
deal to sell the entire parcel for $3,000 to an

Salesmen wait for customers on Sunset near Doheny
Drive. To this day, "star maps" are big sellers.

parents with 16 shotgun blasts, setting off
one of the city's most notorious murder trials. Juries were initially deadlocked after
the brothers raised a defense of sexual
molestation, but Lyle and Erik Menendez
were found guilty in subsequent trials and
sentenced to lifelong prison terms. Before
these tragic events, previous owners of the
house, at separate times, had included pop
stars Elton John and Michael Jackson.

Anglo neighbor, Benjamin Davis Wilson, who became the first American mayor of Los Angeles. His partner in the deal was Major Henry Hancock, who owned the adjacent Rancho La Brea and its tar pits.

Their subsequent attempts to grow wheat were scuttled by drought, and an era of oil drilling yielded dry holes. The area was deemed useless for anything but sheep grazing and vegetable growing, until Burton Green came along and turned it into Beverly Hills. One of the city's founders, oil executive M.H. Whittier, built a stately 38-room mansion on the site.

In 1978, flush with cash from sky-high oil prices of the early 1970s, a Saudi Arabian sheik purchased the estate for $2.5 million. He painted it a color neighbors called "liver bile green" and topped it with a shiny copper roof. But that wasn't what really upset people. On the property wall running directly alongside Sunset Boulevard, a line of Roman-style, nude white statues topped the fence posts. Inexplicably, the shiek decorated them in flesh tones and had their pubic areas painted in realistic or scream-

ing bright colors. The "dirty Disneyland," as it was dubbed, caused an uproar, not to mention traffic jams along Sunset as rubberneckers poured in for a look. The city posted "No Parking" signs, to no avail. The sheik threw a lavish party to appease the neighbors, but it didn't solve the problem of the offending statues.

Rumors then surfaced of troubles in the family and strange goings-on. Work ceased on the remodeling, and the family left. But the flamboyant statues remained, standing like bizarre sentries along Sunset. In 1980, fire gutted the mansion, and still the statues stood there. Finally, the house was sold,

bulldozed, and removed. And finally the statues were gone.

In the years since, these expansive—and expensive— grounds in a prime Beverly Hills location have stood bare—a strange coda to a stranger history.

PLAYBOY MANSION (10236 Charing Cross Road, south of Sunset). Perhaps L.A.'s most notorious party house, this 23-room English Stone Manor was built in 1927 by Arthur Letts Jr., whose father founded both the Broadway and Bullock's department stores. Magazine publisher Hugh Hefner bought it in 1971 and turned it into the Playboy Mansion West, complete with pool, grotto, and a small menagerie of monkeys, peacocks, and exotic birds. Sexual high jinks and endless festivities ensued. Since the grounds are frequently used for special events, there are many, many people in Los Angeles and beyond who can

Guides to the homes of the stars have been best sellers since their inception in the 1920s. Above: Colorful map covers from two eras. Opposite: This winding stretch of Sunset Boulevard, just west of Groverton Place, inspired the Jan and Dean song "Dead Man's Curve."

claim to have partied at the Playboy Mansion.

10000 SUNSET BOULEVARD (south side, with bronze figures). The whimsical bronze statues on the lawn of this estate poke fun at the looky-loo tradition in this neighborhood. One pair resembles sightseers eagerly peering over the fence. Not surprising, since past owners of the house have included Judy Garland, Vincente Minelli, and Howard Hughes.

JAYNE MANSFIELD "PINK PALACE" (10100 Sunset, at Carolwood Drive). In the early 1960s, busty blonde starlet Jayne Mansfield bought this 18-room mansion, built in 1935 by singer Rudy Vallee. She painted it pink and built a heart-shaped pool with an inscription painted on the bottom in cursive: "I love you, Jaynie." Mansfield died in a 1967 crash on a rainy road in a car full of liquor bottles. Singer Engelbert Humperdinck later bought the house for $2 million. In 2001, he

Tempting the Fates

In 1964, surf-singing duo Jan and Dean had a hit song with "Dead Man's Curve," which described a westbound race down Sunset, starting in Hollywood and tearing through the Strip and Beverly Hills. At the deadly curve—just west of Groverton Place and across from UCLA's Drake Stadium—the hero wipes out and dies.

In a famously bizarre case of life imitating art, Jan Berry of the songwriting duo suffered a devastating crash near this very stretch of Sunset in 1966, two years after the record was released. He was driving a Corvette Stringray, just as in the song, when he collided head-on with a gardener's truck. He survived, but sustained severe head injuries that put his career on hold for years while he struggled to recover.

put it on the market for $4.75 million.

The little cul-de-sac it occupies has long been a celebrity magnet. At the end of the short street, visible through a sumptuous wrought-iron gate, sits 141 Carolwood, the elegant Mediterranean mansion built in the 1920s by oilman William Keck. It was later owned by Joseph Schenck, co-founder of 20th Century Fox studios. Aspiring starlet Marilyn Monroe lived there briefly in 1949, sharing the 72-year-old Schenck's boudoir as part of her journey to the top. Since then, Tony Curtis and then-wife Janet Leigh, and later, Sonny and Cher, have owned the home.

ROXBURY DRIVE (the blocks just north and south of Sunset, between Lomitas Avenue and Benedict Canyon Drive). This is perhaps the most famous of all of Beverly Hills' residential streets. For decades, particularly from the 1930s to the 1950s, Roxbury Drive was home to a host of entertainment superstars.

Comedian Jack Benny's colonial-style home at 1002 North Roxbury was among the most famous; he turned the constant sight-seeing into a gag on his TV show by boarding a tourist bus as if it were public transit, to ride it to his own house. His neighbors next door at 1000 North Roxbury were Lucille Ball and Desi Arnaz; long after

Check it out: Beverly Hills

Food and Drink

Polo Lounge (in the Beverly Hills Hotel), 9641 Sunset Boulevard, (310) 276-2251. Elegant dining in historic canteen of the stars and deal-makers—so you can say you've done it.

Spago Beverly Hills, 176 North Canon Drive, (310) 385-0880. Wolfgang Puck's celebrity eatery migrated here from original Sunset Strip location.

The Grill on the Alley, 9560 Dayton Way, (310) 276-0615. Old-school Beverly Hills eatery serving classic American cuisine and signature martinis in dark wood booths with white table-cloths. The deal-making gets heavy at lunchtime.

Nate 'n Al Delicatessen and Restaurant, 414 North Beverly Drive, (310) 274-0101.

Since1940s, where stars and locals alike gather for big breakfasts and Jewish comfort food.

Chadwick, 267 South Beverly Drive, (310) 205-9424. A new "in" spot for serious foodies, focusing on fresh, imaginative California cuisine in season, presented in a cozy, converted house. Chef Ben Ford (son of movie star Harrison) trained at Berkeley's Chez Panisse. Full bar, smashing desserts.

Trolley Tours

On Saturdays only, in July and August through Labor Day, the city provides 40-minute trolley tours of the Beverly Hills business and residential district. Tours depart on the hour, between noon and 5 p.m., from the corner of Rodeo Drive and Dayton Way. Cost is $5. Information: (310) 285-2438.

they split up, she died at this address in 1989. Jimmy Stewart lived in a Tudor-style mansion at 918 North Roxbury, and endured so many gawkers that once, when a family had the gall to lay out a picnic on his front lawn, he walked outside and wordlessly turned on the sprinklers. (After Stewart died on the premises in 1997, his house was razed and a new one erected by the property's subsequent owners.)

A remarkable parade of talent lived at 1019 North Roxbury, beginning with crooner Russ Columbo, who was giving Bing Crosby a run for his money until he was accidentally shot to death in this house with a dueling pistol in 1934. Legendary composers George and Ira Gershwin moved in and wrote some of their best-loved songs here, including "Nice Work If You Can Get It" and "Let's Call the Whole Thing Off," before George died of a brain tumor in 1937. Ira was too upset to continue living in the house, and moved next door to 1021 North Roxbury, where he kept working, writing the lyrics to classic songs like "Old Man River." Singer Rosemary Clooney moved into 1019 with husband Jose Ferrer in 1953, and the house became a popular party spot.

No Ordinary High School

The oil well pumping away at the corner of the property is just one clue this is no ordinary high school—another is the student parking lot full of new Audis, Jeeps, and BMWs. With its smaller class sizes, stellar facilities, and exceptional test scores, a seat in this school is so sought after that parents are required to sign sworn affidavits of residency, and a team of investigators throws out an average of 100 impostors a year.

Still, attendance at Beverly Hills High is no guarantee of a glowing future—witness the escapades of former students Monica Lewinsky, the world's most famous White House intern, and brothers Lyle and Erik Menendez, who are now spending their post-grad days in prison for

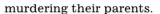

Above: Aerial photo of the Beverly Hills High School campus, from 1995. Century City flanks the school on its western edge. Right: BHHS students Rob Reiner, Albert Brooks (then known as Albert Einstein), and Richard Dreyfuss, from 1964.

murdering their parents.

Alumni the school is prouder to claim include Alicia Silverstone (her starring role in *Clueless* was, indeed, pop culture imitating life), Carrie Fisher, Nicolas Cage, David Schwimmer, Shaun Cassidy, Larraine Newman, Marlo Thomas, Rob Reiner, Albert Brooks, Julie Kavner, Joel Grey, Richard Dreyfuss, and Betty White.

Many students are the offspring of celebrities, giving them a head start that can be further exploited at a school that offers, in addition to a planetarium and science lab, three theaters, a radio station, a closed-circuit television station, and facilities for producing a film from start to finish.

Tucked into a residential area south of the Golden Triangle commercial district, this off-the-beaten-track campus is worth a look for its charming architecture and lovely 26 acres. Just don't expect to match the location to a certain long-running television show. That was set at a "West Beverly High School" and filmed elsewhere. And at the real Beverly Hills High, the postal code is 90212. ⊜

Bel-Air, UCLA, and Brentwood

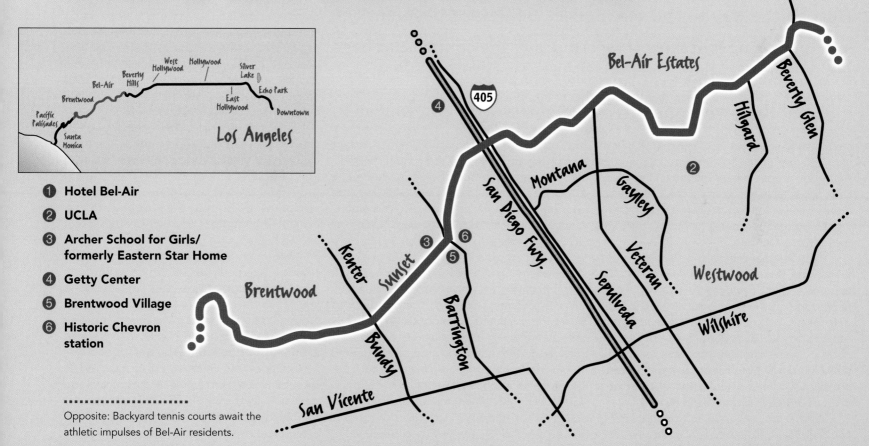

Los Angeles

1. **Hotel Bel-Air**
2. **UCLA**
3. **Archer School for Girls/ formerly Eastern Star Home**
4. **Getty Center**
5. **Brentwood Village**
6. **Historic Chevron station**

Opposite: Backyard tennis courts await the athletic impulses of Bel-Air residents.

Bel-Air

From its midpoint in Beverly

Hills all the way to the sea, Sunset Boulevard becomes the stuff of driving fantasies, a twisting, curving course that begs to be navigated in a fast, top-down roadster.

Combined with the lure of celebrity dwelling places in

such fabled enclaves as Bel-Air and Brentwood, the boulevard's wide-swinging angles make for a potentially lethal setup. More than a few fatal accidents have taken place along this treacherous stretch, leading the city to regrade a number of curves over the last several decades.

Past the intersection at Beverly Glen Boulevard, Sunset slices between the UCLA campus and the exclusive Bel-Air residential neighborhood. On the left is the youthful and democratic vibe of California's largest public university, with its jogging paths and tennis courts; on the right are the "stay away" signals emanating from the stone gates and ivy-covered walls encircling one of the city's most prestigious residential quarters.

Farther on, beyond the bridge crossing the San Diego Freeway, Sunset enters leafy and picturesque Brentwood, which is fast becoming the place where real estate values are highest of all among the fabled "3 B's" (the others being Beverly Hills and Bel-Air) on celebrity star maps. At this point, ocean air and fog signal the beginnings, at last, of relative proximity to the beach.

In Bel-Air, it's often said, the air is 10 degrees cooler and the oxygen richer than in much of the rest of Los Angeles. This may actually be true, thanks to the profusion of flowering trees and greenery that shade the streets and scent the breezes in this exclusive, glade-like neighborhood, aptly named in the early 1920s by its founder, oil-rich developer Alphonzo E. Bell.

Fewer than 10,000 residents share Bel-Air's coveted 90007 postal code, yet it looms large as the chosen dwelling place of some of the richest and most exotic denizens of Los Angeles.

Who are the people who live here? Oil men and hoteliers, dotty old heiresses and champion athletes, movie stars, directors, producers and screenwriters, investment bankers and land barons, plastic surgeons and TV stars, an ex-president and first lady, corporate fat cats, top litigators, and the occasional rock star, to name a few.

Discretion is prized in a community of walled estates, splendid isolation, and rustic canyon views, where the country club golf course is one of the few places local life forms are ever publicly spotted. But the seal of privacy is occasionally breached by reports of a jaw-dropping real estate transaction.

One such deal was a complex $60-million wampum swap in September 2000 involving various properties that included the 1930s estate of the late hotel magnate Conrad Hilton, which featured, among other amenities, a doghouse with its own fountain and garden. Harder to sell has been the exotic ridge-top love nest of the late basketball great Wilt Chamberlain, designed in the 1970s as a playground for his reputed 20,000 sexual conquests. Even after more than a year on the market and a

This romantic restaurant terrace at the Hotel Bel-Air has inspired countless marriage proposals. Weddings often follow on the grounds.

$3-million price reduction, to $4.3 million by the summer of 2001, the kinky castle was still too unique to find a taker. But despite its members-only image, not *every* house in "the 007" carries an exceptional price tag; according to one area Realtor, the range in the summer of 2001 scraped bottom at around $450,000, usually for the

rare stucco clunker built in the 1960s.

But Bel-Air isn't for everyone who can afford it. Some find its lack of shops and nearby conveniences distressing. Its opulent stone gates, once closed to all but residents, are now merely showpieces that anyone can drive through, leaving the community readily accessible to gawkers and Sunday drivers. But, in truth, there's little to draw outsiders beyond the lovely bar and restaurant at the Hotel Bel-Air.

Located about a mile north of Sunset

on Stone Canyon Road, a sun-dappled lane thickly shaded by overhanging trees, the historic hotel played a central role in the development of the community, much as happened in Beverly Hills. Its lobby was originally a real estate office from which residential lots were sold in the 1920s. (The two hotels have something else in common—they're owned by brothers from the royal family of the tiny, petroleum-rich country of Brunei.)

It's commonly said that oil built Bel-Air, just as surely as a lack of oil built Beverly Hills. But the oil was discovered in Santa Fe Springs, where gentleman farmer Alphonzo Bell hit a gusher in 1921 that made him extremely wealthy—for some years, he reputedly earned up to $300,000 *a month* from his lucky strike.

Bell used some of the money to buy a 4,500-acre ranch with a house at the top of present-day Bel-Air Road and set about subdividing his acreage. Much like Burton Green in Beverly Hills, he envisioned a suburban development that would appeal exclusively to the rich—and thus set a high bar for the minimum amount that could be spent on building a home there. In 1923, Bell set the amount at the then considerable sum of $10,000.

The Bel-Air land office (at the present Hotel Bel-Air) opened for business in 1922. The surrounding streets were fully landscaped from the start and given names—Bellagio, Perugia, Stradella, and Portofino— inspired by the Italian travels of Bell's wife.

Originally, Bell prohibited sales to movie industry folk, fearing their presence would bring a disruptive stream of looky-loos. But his resistance soon faded. A record published by the Bel-Air Association shows that Clark Gable, at the height of his fame, was courted to buy a five-acre site. When extended location filming took Gable out of the running, the site was purchased by producer Victor Fleming, who built on it and moved in. Filmmaker Howard Hawks and his wife, Slim, later built a house on a 95-acre site and became an integral part of the community.

Bell's real estate development activities made him even richer than had his oil strike. He also developed the Bel-Air Bay Club and Bel-Air Country Club, along with various areas in Pacific Palisades. Along the way, he became a tennis champion, civic leader, and philanthropist. His son, Alphonzo E. Bell Jr., was elected to Congress.

By 1946, Bell's sales office had served its purpose. An associate, Joe Drown, envisioned a second life for the building as part of a garden-style hotel, and supervised the renovations as well as the landscaping.

Painted pink and white, the Mission-style hotel, at 701 Stone Canyon Road, has epitomized the flavor of the neighborhood for more than 50 years. Privacy, tranquility, and superlative service are its hallmarks. Its one-story suites and buildings are scattered coyly among garden paths lush with plantings of bird of paradise, roses, camellias, gardenias, and flowering peaches.

Guests enter across a fairy-tale stone

....

The Bel-Air Country Club, shown in 1929, was among many real estate development projects undertaken by the area's oil-rich founder, Alphonzo E. Bell, who took advantage of the facilities to become a champion tennis player.

bridge over a rustic stream, while white swans preen in an adjacent pond. The 12-acre grounds include a 40-foot oval swimming pool, koi pond, soaring trees, and extensive herb garden. The 92 individually decorated rooms and suites include fireplaces, floral arrangements, in-room tea service, and, in some cases, private tiled patios, fountains, and Jacuzzis.

The hotel bar is a cozy hideaway with a roaring fireplace, patterned on an English hunting lodge. Humphrey Bogart was a regular in the 1940s. It later became a hangout for Frank Sinatra, Dean Martin, and the rest of the Rat Pack.

The restaurant's dining room has accommodated many a movie deal or business alliance. The real draw, though, is the outdoor terrace, where bougainvillea petals drift down from the arbors in summer. In winter, subtle warmth emanates from heaters beneath the patio tiles. It's the ultimate ladies' lunch spot, favored at least once a week by former First Lady Nancy Reagan, who lives nearby on St. Cloud Road, and her pal, department store heiress Betsy Bloomingdale.

By night, the romantic aspects of the terrace have inspired many a marriage proposal. Weddings follow, with the grounds hosting as many as five ceremonies a weekend in high season.

Celebrities are frequently in residence. In earlier times, Grace Kelly, David Niven, and Sir Laurence Olivier checked in, along with Cary Grant, Marilyn Monroe, and Elizabeth Taylor. When the disastrous Bel-Air fire threatened the hotel in 1961, Gore Vidal and director Otto Preminger were among the guests flushed out in an evacuation.

More recently, guests have included Julia Roberts, Robin Williams, Tom Cruise and Nicole Kidman, and Robert De Niro, who threw a birthday party for his six-year-old son here, with Billy Crystal entertaining and Whoopi Goldberg dishing out ice cream. On a recent visit, rock star Neil Young was seen slouching toward the pool, wrapped in a bathrobe and shades, prior to playing a concert that night further east on Sunset at the Hollywood Palladium. And the sense of escape from care is so pervasive that a significant percentage of guests have local addresses. For years, actor Tony Curtis has divided his time between the hotel and another home in Hawaii.

In all, the place has the capacity to throw its guests into a narcotized trance of luxury and pleasure. The only antidote, apparently, is the threat of a rapidly mounting bill, and to many, even that has no significance at all.

Among the well-known addresses found in the curving streets north of Sunset are:

668 ST. CLOUD ROAD—Ronald and Nancy Reagan moved in after leaving the White House in 1988. Their 6,500-square-foot ranch house, hidden behind a security fence and guard gate, was a gift from political supporters, who purchased it for them for $2.5 million in 1987. The house number was 666 until Nancy had it changed, aware that the number signifies the Antichrist in the Book of Revelations.

750 BEL AIR ROAD—This is the former site of a house that drew sightseers for many years when it doubled as the Clampett mansion in the long-running TV series "The Beverly Hillbillies." Built in 1935 by Lyman Atkinson, an engineer who designed the Hoover Dam before striking it rich in oil, the house featured one bathroom with gold oil derricks for water faucets. Because Atkinson's wife hated the house and refused to move in, the family never resided there. The home was later purchased by television producer Jerry Perenchio, who tore it down, combined the land with that of two other estates, and built a new mansion.

938 BEL AIR ROAD—Actress Zsa Zsa Gabor, the self-crowned "Queen of Bel-Air," renovated this old mansion formerly owned by Howard Hughes.

594 SOUTH MAPLETON DRIVE—In the 1980s, television producer Aaron Spelling ("Charlie's Angels," "Dynasty," "Beverly Hills 90210") and wife Candy raised the bar for ostentatious displays of wealth when they built this 56,500-square-foot house, dubbed "The Manor." It covers an area the size of a football field and has its own skating rink, tennis court, bowling alley, and swimming pool.

232 SOUTH MAPLETON DRIVE—Lovebird movie stars Humphrey Bogart and Lauren Bacall lived here after they married, until he died of cancer in 1957.

11001 SUNSET BOULEVARD—Truman Capote died here in August 1984 while a houseguest of Joanna Carson, ex-wife of talk show host Johnny. The author died of liver failure after a three-day drug-and-drinking binge.

10957 BELLAGIO ROAD—Movie maker Alfred Hitchcock lived here for more than 40 years with wife Alma and their daughter, until his death at age 81 from heart failure in April 1980. He rented another home visible across the golf course of the

Bel-Air Country Club for his *Rear Window* star Grace Kelly. Always peculiar, Hitchcock liked to brag that Kelly, a regal blonde, shared his inclination toward voyeurism and allowed him to watch her

private activities through a telescope in his den.

685 STONE CANYON ROAD—This is where movie producer Don Simpson (*Top Gun, Beverly Hills Cop, Days of Thunder*) lived out the high-octane lifestyle and drug-fueled escapades that made him a legend, of sorts, until he was found nude on the bathroom floor, dead of a drug overdose, at 52.

STONE CANYON RESERVOIR—Although inaccessible to the public, this fenced-off water source at the top of Stone Canyon Road was the location used in the movie *Chinatown* as the fictional "Oak Pass Reservoir," where water commissioner Hollis Mulwray is found dead. In another scene shot here, private eye Jake Gittes (Jack Nicholson) gets his nose sliced by a thug (director Roman Polanski) for poking it around in the wrong place.

••••••••••••••••••••

A star map vendor along Sunset Boulevard makes another sale.

The Bel-Air/Brentwood Fire

Bel-Air's stone gates couldn't keep out tragedy on an autumn day in 1961. On November 6, wind-whipped sparks and flaming debris from a rubbish fire on a construction site in Sherman Oaks were sent aloft across the Santa Monica Mountains. Within minutes, flaming embers were dancing across wood-shingled rooftops in the canyons of Bel-Air and Brentwood, igniting the most devastating fire in the history of Los Angeles.

Although battled by 2,500 firefighters, the inferno raged for 12 hours and destroyed 484 homes. Police officers evacuated 3,500 residents. Remarkably, no one was killed.

Headlined "A Tragedy Trimmed in Mink" by *Life* magazine, the fire made Bel-Air and Brentwood famous, as television viewers across the country watched well-known personalities scrambling to save their homes.

Richard Nixon, who had just lost a presidential race to John F. Kennedy, jumped onto the roof of his rented house with a garden hose to wet down the shingles before escaping with Checkers, his cocker spaniel. Bandleader Lawrence Welk stayed up on the roof all night at his home on Tiger-

Right: Zsa Zsa Gabor enlists a friend to help sift for jewels in the rubble of her Bel-Air home. Far right: Houses along Chalon Road are reduced to matchsticks in the 1961 blaze.

tail Road, fending off flames with a hose. Fred MacMurray and Maureen O'Hara took up similar positions.

Attorney Everett Laybourne was trying a case in court when the clerk gave him a message: "Your house is on fire." He raced home to find his abode in the 1000 block of Roscomare Road engulfed in 50-foot flames. Alfred Hitchcock was among those who stood in the road comforting neighbors.

Burt Lancaster lost his house, but not his art collection, as he had it on loan to the Los Angeles County Museum of Art. Zsa Zsa Gabor was shown on television, sifting through the ashes with a shovel to look for her jewels, while sporting a 10-carat diamond on one finger.

Residents still remember the terror, the anxiety, the sirens, and the heat—and the sense of devastation when possessions and

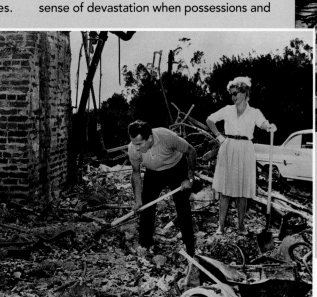

keepsakes were wiped out.

Then-Governor Pat Brown declared Los Angeles a disaster area, and the fire was put down as the worst in a single California community since the great San Francisco fire of 1906.

UCLA

The most popular university in the nation is located right on Sunset Boulevard.

For nearly half a mile starting at Hilgard Avenue, Sunset forms the northern border of the campus of the University of California, Los Angeles, a virtual "city within a city," with

some 163 buildings on its 419-acre campus. Open to visitors, the campus accommodates more than 36,000 students enrolled annually, making it the largest university in California, public or private. In 2001, it was also the most popular university in the nation for the third straight year with more than 37,000 students applying for 4,200 slots in the previous fall's freshman class.

UCLA started as a teachers' college in downtown Los Angeles in 1919 on the site of the present-day Central Library. By the late 1920s, the growing school needed a new home

....

Opposite: The UCLA campus in 1930. Sunset Boulevard curves along between the buildings and the body of water at right—a reservoir that still exists, though smaller now, between Marymount High School and the Bel-Air Country Club.

and found it here at the former Wolfskill Ranch, on land that had once belonged to the Mexican governor. Ground was broken for the new campus on September 21, 1927.

The first four buildings completed, in 1929, still form the heart of the old campus—including Royce Hall, with its distinctive, much-photographed tower, and Powell Library, standing across from each other on the grassy Quad. Both are modeled in the Romanesque style of

14th century northern Italy, impressively crafted in red brick with striped facades and ornate features.

Royce Hall, designed by architect David Allison, was patterned on the Church of San Ambrogio in Milan. Its open-air loggia features ceiling frescoes that depict "The Instruction of the World" by 12 notable teachers, including Christ, Socrates, Plato, Aristotle, Kant, Darwin, and Einstein. The main feature is a 1,900-seat central auditorium, which is regularly used for public concerts and special events. Opera singer

UNIVERSITY OF CALIFORNIA AT LOS ANGELES, WESTWOOD HILLS, CALIFORNIA

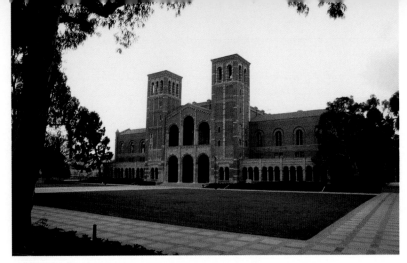

Luciano Pavarotti made his American debut here, and the Los Angeles Philharmonic has used it for recording sessions.

Powell Library, designed by George Kelham, features an octagonal tower patterned on the Church of St. Sepolcro in Bologna, Italy, and a main entrance modeled after the Church of San Zenove in Verona. Beneath an interior dome 63 feet high, it features some 150,000 volumes and 800 reading seats.

Nearby Haines and Kinsey halls, which house classrooms, are the other two original buildings.

Visitors often gravitate to Ackerman Student Union, the five-story striped brick structure in the central campus that houses an information booth, food courts, and an enormous bookstore selling UCLA clothing and souvenirs along with art supplies, software, and other materials.

On the plaza near Ackerman stands the Bruin Bear, a 10-foot-long, two-ton bronze grizzly that has served as a landmark and meeting post since it was placed there by the alumni association in 1984.

The Franklin D. Murphy Sculpture Garden on the northern side of the campus also draws many visitors. More than 70 works by 20th century sculptors such as Rodin, Calder, Matisse, Miro, and Nogushi are on permanent display in the grassy, open-air quadrangle in front of Bunche Hall, a popular place to lounge and study.

Art, film, theater, music, and other performing arts programs on the campus attract more than half a million visitors each year, and many others come for basketball games at Pauley Pavilion, tennis tournaments, and other sporting events.

UCLA spent its first 20 years as a fairly modest campus—there were only 14 buildings until the late 1940s. But after World War II, it began to grow rapidly along with the rest of Los Angeles, and construction was constant from the 1950s through the mid-1970s. By the late 1970s, UCLA had passed its oldest sister in the UC system, Berkeley, in enrollment. Its film school was coming into its own at around the same time. UCLA has the second-largest film and television archive in the world.

The UCLA Extension program of night and weekend classes for non-degree students is the largest in the nation, offering more than 4,500 courses to 100,000 enrollees each quarter.

Today, UCLA estimates that one in every 140 Californians has earned a degree from the campus, giving it a remarkable influence on the growth and development of the state.

Brentwood

Coming out of Bel-Air

headed west, Sunset Boulevard crosses The Great Divide—the roaring 405, or San Diego Freeway, which has bisected the hills and canyons through the Sepulveda Pass ever since it was constructed in the late 1950s.

Visible from the bridge over the freeway is the world-famous Getty Center arts complex, resplendent in white travertine limestone on the hill to the north. Entering Brentwood, Sunset slips westward through the greenery of a stretch with a country club atmosphere. Tennis, anyone? Golf? Riding? Equestrian trails and stables characterize Sullivan Canyon, just off Sunset.

The deluxe residences along this section of the boulevard resemble those in

••••••••••••••••••••••

The elegant 1931 Eastern Star Home fronts on Sunset Boulevard. The former retirement facility has become a school for girls. Opposite, left: UCLA's Royce Hall hosts countless music and cultural events. Opposite, right: The headless sculpture, Rodin's "Walking Man," is among 70 outdoor artworks displayed at the Franklin D. Murphy Sculpture Garden.

Bel-Air and Beverly Hills, while slightly further on, apartment complexes pop up as evidence of Brentwood's more democratic character. Remarkably, median home sale prices in Brentwood now outstrip those of both Bel-Air and Beverly Hills. The area's ocean proximity, its flatter, family-friendly streets, and convenient, "village" lifestyle have increased its popularity among homebuyers,

according to Realtors. Among the movers and shakers who call Brentwood home are former Los Angeles mayor Richard Riordan, billionaire developer and philanthropist Eli Broad, and mega talent manager and former CAA head Mike Ovitz.

Brentwood has a history of deal-makers—it takes its name from a prominent attorney, Lancaster Brent, who acquired much of the land in lieu of legal fees from one of Los Angeles' earliest Spanish land grant settlers, Señora Arcadia Bandini Baker. Around the turn of the century, he

sold it to developer Robert C. Gillis, who later annexed it to the city of Los Angeles. Earlier still, the lands were occupied by Tongva Indians, who were forced by the Spaniards to join the San Gabriel Mission in the 1770s.

As Sunset travels its way west, the boulevard acquires the feel of a large residential thoroughfare that is only occasionally interrupted with pockets of shops. The Getty Center houses its scholars in residence in a striking apartment complex at 11781 Sunset Boulevard, just west of Barrington Avenue, that was designed by the late architect Paul Williams, who also made key renovations to the Beverly Hills Hotel.

Among other landmarks in this stretch is the former Eastern Star Home, at 11725 Sunset. Built in 1933 as a retirement home and convalescent facility, the elegant Spanish Colonial Mission-style building, with its rose gardens and fountains, was used as the fictional Mar Vista Inn and Rest Home in the movie *Chinatown*. In a memorable

....

This sign at Mount St. Mary's College alerts motorists to watch for nuns. Opposite: Spectacular sunsets, shown above, and the flora and fauna of the Central Garden, below, enhance the experience for Getty Center visitors.

scene, private eye Jake Gittes (Jack Nicholson) visits the elderly residents to uncover a land-laundering scam and gets slugged in the face before Faye Dunaway comes roaring up the circular drive to help him escape. In 1998, the home was converted to serve as the private Archer School for Girls in grades seven through 12.

Two miles north of Sunset off Bundy Drive is the Chalon Road campus of Mount St. Mary's College, built in 1925. With its 16th century Spanish-style buildings on 56 pastoral acres, it's one of the prettiest campuses in California and frequently used in filming.

The Chevron filling station at the southeast corner of Sunset and Barrington is an official cultural historic landmark, built in 1938 by architect Raymond Stockdale, and the only Spanish Colonial-style gas station in Los Angeles. Its 40-foot tower houses a

spacious room that was rented in the 1950s and 1960s by writers who liked its solitude and views. Screenwriter James Poe used the room to write the movies *Lilies of the Field*; *They Shoot Horses, Don't They?*; and *Around the World in 80 Days*, an adaptation for which he shared an Oscar in 1956.

The tiny Brentwood Village shopping area at Sunset and Barrington opened in 1949, along with the local post office. Movie star Gary Cooper, a longtime Brentwood resident (his estate was just off Sunset behind St. Martin of Tours Catholic Church) was named honorary mayor in 1949, and rode a magnificent palomino horse through a crowd of 4,000 people to receive the mayor's mantle. The Brent-Air Pharmacy, still family owned and operated, opened in 1951. More recently the village has attracted some upscale shops and restaurants.

The Getty Center

Reached by riding a winding, uphill tram from the parking area, this splendid $1-billion arts complex put Brentwood on the world map when it opened in late 1997. Its vast collection, funded by the trust of the late oil tycoon J. Paul Getty, includes modern photography, pre-20th century European paintings, and a vast collection of antiquities. Its galleries are housed in five interconnected two-story pavilions featuring sky-lit upper levels. Among the highlights are Van Gogh's "Irises," Degas' "After the Bath," Cezanne's "Still Life With Apples," Mantegna's "Adoration of the Magi," and works by Rembrandt, da Vinci, Titian, Renoir, Monet, Goya, and Brueghel. The research and conservation institutes and libraries of the J. Paul Getty Trust are also here, along with an auditorium, bookstore, gift shop, restaurant, and two cafes.

For many visitors, the building itself and its plaza, gardens, and city views are a bigger draw than what's inside. Architect Richard Meier used rough-textured, guillotine-cut Italian travertine, an off-white limestone at least 8,000 years old, containing the fossilized remains of leaves and fish, as the material for a stunning complex of low-lying geometric buildings clustered along the natural ridges of the hilltop site. Particularly at sunset, views of the Pacific Ocean, San Gabriel Mountains, and city sprawl are dramatic and available from various stairways and from the Central Garden. The much-heralded garden was designed by Robert Irwin with a zigzagging path down to a circular pond surrounded by azaleas, bougainvillea, hydrangea, and fruit trees.

Always free to the public, aside from a $5 parking fee, the museum was such a hit its first year that administrators were compelled to take out ads discouraging attendance. Since then, the museum has been broadening its outreach with populist events such as free movies, concerts by unsigned local rock bands, and a conference on 1960s and 1970s Pop artists that drew the glitterati of the West Coast art scene.

The Getty Center is at 1200 Getty Center Drive off the San Diego Freeway. Closed Mondays, open 10 a.m. to 7 p.m. Tuesday and Wednesday, 10 a.m. to 9 p.m. Thursdays and Fridays, 10 a.m. to 6 p.m. weekends. Information and parking reservations: (310) 440-7300.

The true commercial heart of Brentwood lies along San Vicente Boulevard, a thriving strip best reached by turning left at Barrington or Bundy, then right at the intersection several blocks south of Sunset. Planted with distinctive coral trees and bisected by a broad green median, San Vicente is popular with runners and dog-walkers. The street continues all the way to the bluffs above the ocean, about three miles west. In Brentwood, San Vicente is lined with juice bars and gyms, coffee shops, trendy restaurants and expensive boutiques, and epitomizes the laid-back but active, physically oriented lifestyle that many people associate with Los Angeles' upscale Westside communities.

The busy Starbucks at San Vicente and Kenter Avenue is usually abuzz with gym-toned actor-waiters who congregate on the low wall outside, trading talk about jobs and night life. In this high-density district of condos and apartment houses, Brentwood has a thick population of young professionals and strivers in the arts, sports, health, and retail worlds. Residents often speak of the open, familiar "village" feel fostered at various community hubs, including the quaint Brentwood Country Mart, at San Vicente and 26th Street, and the well-regarded independent bookstore Dutton's Brentwood, at 11975 San Vicente near Bundy.

Of course, few people can drive through Brentwood without recalling the notorious O.J. Simpson murder trial and the media attention that overwhelmed the neighborhood after the stabbing deaths of Nicole Brown Simpson and Ronald Goldman in June 1994. This is the neighborhood where the athlete/actor and Nicole lived and frolicked before their marriage dissolved, and where Goldman worked as a waiter at Mezzaluna (a restaurant at 11700 San Vicente) and met Nicole for the first time at the Starbucks at Kenter. It's where Brown and Goldman were stabbed to death on the doorstep of her condo (875 South Bundy Drive), and where Simpson was arrested at his mansion (360 Rockingham Avenue) in connection with the double murder.

The sensational events galvanized worldwide media attention, causing an invasion of the neighborhood by tourists, press, and looky-loos that lasted nearly four years. A fed-up resident finally erected a huge sign on Bundy that declared "Go Home—There is Nothing 2 See!"

And by now, there really isn't. Simpson, held liable for the killings in a civil trial and fined $33.5 million, sold his Rockingham manse to help pay off his debts, and left town with his children. The new owner demolished the house in 1998. Mezzaluna, unable to shake the morbid publicity, closed in 1997 and was replaced by a Peet's coffeehouse. Nicole Brown's condo has been sold and re-landscaped. Still, the lore of those addresses remains, unlikely to lose its hold on visitors who spent years caught up in the suspense of the unfolding murder saga and its cast of characters.

Here are additional addresses of Brentwood residents who have captured their share of attention:

12305 FIFTH HELENA—The modest bungalow where Marilyn Monroe was secluded on August 5, 1962, when she died

The cottage where Marilyn Monroe breathed her last.

of a drug overdose that was ruled a suicide.

12216 SHETLAND LANE—Raymond Chandler lived here in the 1940s, while writing the novels *High Window* and *Lady of the Lake*, as well as the screenplay for *Double Indemnity*.

426 NORTH BRISTOL—Joan Crawford bought this elegant showplace in 1929, and lived here with Doug Fairbanks when he married her after leaving Mary Pickford. In her book *Mommie Dearest*, Crawford's daughter Christina describes living here in an atmosphere of alcoholic rages and terror. The movie starring Faye Dunaway did not use this house as a location; by then it was owned by actor Donald O'Connor.

231 NORTH ROCKINGHAM ROAD—Growing up as a phenomenally popular child star, Shirley Temple lived in this house with her family. The dimpled moppet had her own little cottage complete with a working soda fountain. She later returned to the house and moved in with her first husband.

513 MORENO AVENUE—Where gangster Mickey Cohen lived, adjacent to the Brentwood Country Club, in relative peace and quiet until a bomb planted by gangland enemies rocked the neighborhood and left a crater six feet deep. Cohen survived the attack and calmly posed for newspaper photographers in his bathrobe. ⓢ

Check it out: Bel-Air, UCLA, and Brentwood

Food and Drink

Cafe at Dutton's (in Dutton's Brentwood Books), 11975 San Vicente Drive, Brentwood, (310) 476-6263. Coffee, pastries, sandwiches.

El Dorado, 11777 San Vicente Boulevard, Brentwood, (310) 207-0150. Upscale Mexican cuisine, lively bar, great desserts.

Four Oaks, 2181 North Beverly Glen Boulevard, (310) 470-2265. Upscale country-cottage hideaway, California-French cuisine, in Bel-Air/Westwood area.

Hotel Bel-Air restaurant and bar, 701 Stone Canyon Road, (310) 472-1211. California-French cuisine in romantic restaurant plus hunting lodge-style bar in exclusive hideaway hotel setting.

Matteo's, 2321 Westwood Boulevard, Westwood, (310) 475-4521. Popular, convivial Italian joint.

Mojo (in W Hotel), 930 Hilgard Avenue, Westwood, (310) 208-8765. Swank bar and restaurant, creative Nuevo Latino cuisine.

Zen Zoo Tea, 13050 San Vicente Boulevard No. 114 (adjacent to Brentwood Country Mart), (310) 576-0585. 40 kinds of Asian teas, chai, dim sum, edamame, salads. A haven for Asia-philes, health nuts, and seekers of inner bliss.

Additional Interest

University of California, Los Angeles. Campus visitors center, providing maps and information, is at corner of Le Conte and Broxton avenues. (310) 825-4321.

UCLA Hannah Carter Japanese Garden (in Bel-Air), 10619 Bellagio Road, (310) 825-4574. Formal gardens created in 1961 include koi pond, teahouse, five-tiered pagoda, and Hawaiian garden on 1.5 acres. Parking reservations required.

Westwood Farmers Market. Every Thursday, 2-7 p.m., at Westwood Boulevard and Weyburn Avenue. A weekly block party with 70 vendors, jazz band, crafts.

Beachcombers stroll the Malibu oceanfront, about a mile north of Cross Creek Road, in 1989.

Pacific Palisades and the Beach

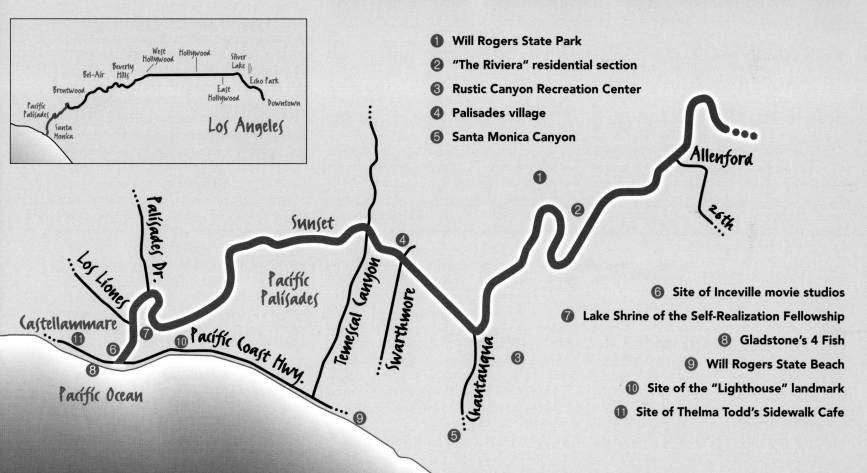

1. Will Rogers State Park
2. "The Riviera" residential section
3. Rustic Canyon Recreation Center
4. Palisades village
5. Santa Monica Canyon

6. Site of Inceville movie studios
7. Lake Shrine of the Self-Realization Fellowship
8. Gladstone's 4 Fish
9. Will Rogers State Beach
10. Site of the "Lighthouse" landmark
11. Site of Thelma Todd's Sidewalk Cafe

West Hollywood
Hollywood
Silver Lake
Bel-Air
Beverly Hills
Brentwood
East Hollywood
Echo Park
Pacific Palisades
Downtown
Santa Monica
Los Angeles

Allenford
26th

Sunset

Palisades Dr.

Los Líones

Pacific Palisades

Temescal Canyon

Swarthmore

Castellammare

Pacific Coast Hwy.

Chautauqua

Pacific Ocean

The Palisades

As it winds along toward its end, Sunset Boulevard curves past tall stands of rustling eucalyptus trees and woodsy canyons on its way through an area named after the sea cliffs that separate it from the ocean: Pacific Palisades. Finally, the beach is close by.

Although the ocean can be reached directly by turning left at Chautauqua Boulevard and going straight through Santa Monica Canyon, taking the short cut may be short-sighted. Sunset has reserved a climactic flourish for its last dash to the sea, and extends its length by following the coast north more than two miles, swinging through hills and canyons, before it finally breaks through to the Pacific.

Residents of this final neighborhood along the way like to maintain that Sunset saves the best for last. Indeed, the Palisades can seem like the village that time forgot—an upscale small town brimming with charm and friendliness, nestled between the beach and the Santa Monica Mountains. From Sunset left at Via de la Paz, it's only a short way to the bluffs,

where storybook houses cluster over world-class ocean views that, by freeway on a good day, are within half an hour of the downtown in one of the world's major cities.

With 23,000 residents, the 90272 postal code has its own newspaper, the *Palisades Times*, and a small but lively commercial strip of restaurants, cafes, boutiques, and shops centered in the blocks around Sunset and Swarthmore Avenue. It's the kind of place where moms and kids all seem to know each other, full of second-, third-, and fourth-generation families with parents who went to "Pali High" and can't imagine raising their kids anywhere else.

Pacific Palisades is also home to some of the town's wealthiest residents and most famous names, including cinema king Steven Spielberg, who lives with wife

Kate Capshaw and their family in an ocean-view compound on Amalfi Drive in the hilltop Riviera section. Among the other residents are Arnold Schwarzenegger and his wife, Maria Shriver; television writer-producer David E. Kelley ("The Practice," "Ally McBeal") and movie-star wife Michelle Pfeiffer; movie producer Brian Grazer; entertainer Bill Cosby; and actor Anthony Hopkins (*Silence of the Lambs, The Remains of the Day*), a long-time resident who was named honorary mayor. Even Dennis Tito, the multimillionaire who booked passage into outer space with the Russians, lives in Pacific Palisades. Come here on a weekend, as many people do to enjoy a village fair or attend a polo match at Will Rogers State Park, and you never know whom you'll see window shopping or eating lunch.

From the beginning, the remoteness and geography of Pacific Palisades have had much to do with its history. For thousands of years, the area was occupied by Tongva natives who came to be called Gabrieliño Indians when the missions were founded. In

•••••••••••••••••••••••

Opposite: Aerial view of Pacific Palisades in the 1930s. Subdividing and homebuilding had accelerated after Sunset Boulevard reached the area a few years earlier.

the 1830s and after, the king of Spain parceled out the land in grants to his Mexican subjects, including Ysidro Reyes and Francisco Marquez, for whom one of the main roads is named.

In the early 1920s, representatives of the Methodist Episcopal Church chose the area, which they had been using for spiritual assemblies, as the site for a residential community based on "Christian ideals and dedicated to peace." On January 14, 1922, a gathering of church members led by the Reverend Charles Scott established a camp under the Founder's Oaks in Temescal Canyon and officially founded Pacific Palisades, with an associa-

tion that leased out lots for home building. Among the founding tenets was that only Anglos would be permitted to own property. To this day, the area is overwhelmingly white.

At first, Angelenos viewed the remote development among the sycamore groves mainly as an area for weekend homes and woodsy retreats. Then, in January 1926, road crews pushed Sunset Boulevard through the hills all the way to the ocean. The area was suddenly far more accessible, and a flood of new homebuilders took an interest. (Sunset was linked with an existing street called Beverly Boulevard, which retained that name until July 1934, when the entire route was unified as Sunset Boulevard to capitalize on the thoroughfare's growing fame.)

Within a short time of the opening ceremonies for the new thoroughfare, people could ride all the way from downtown's Pershing Square to the ocean end of Pacific Palisades on buses that billed the route as "Southern California's Prettiest Drive."

Entertainer Will Rogers was among the first to take advantage of the new access. The cowboy philosopher had already built a polo field and rustic weekend home on his Palisades ranch; in 1928, he moved his per-

884 THE WILL ROGERS' RANCH HOUSE IN THE SANTA MONICA MOUNTAINS, OVERLOOKING THE PACIFIC NOT FAR FROM BEVERLY HILLS, CALIFORNIA

manent home and entire operations there. Rogers had grown up on 60,000 acres in the Indian Territory of Oklahoma, and he said the sage- and chaparral-covered hills near the sea reminded him of his boyhood years.

Palisades neighbors took pride in Rogers' presence; he fit in easily and became a familiar character. Local legend has it that Rogers planted many of the eucalyptus trees along this stretch of Sunset Boulevard. He also spent many an evening hour sitting on a stool at the Santa Monica Canyon drugstore run by his pal, Doc Laws. Rogers would soak up the conversation and concerns of the locals, then use some of the material for his radio broadcasts and writings, which were a source of encouragement to many during the Depression.

His column, "Will Rogers Remarks," which was syndicated on the front page of more than 500 newspapers, offered comical but shrewd observations that endeared him to millions of Americans who felt that Rogers spoke for them, if only they had the gift to put things just that way. Rogers, who was also hugely popular in movie roles, was an avid booster of aviation and a frequent flyer, although never a pilot himself. In 1935, at the height of his career, he was flying over Alaska with a pilot friend, Wiley Post, when the small craft went down and both men were killed. The loss was devastating to his family, including daughter Mary and sons Will Jr. and Jim. They continued to live at the ranch for some years. In 1944, his wife Betty donated the house and 186-acre grounds to the state of California.

Today, a sign on Sunset Boulevard points to Will Rogers State Park, where free tours are conducted of the rustic ranch house, furnished just as it was during Rogers' life. A museum on the grounds features film clips showing Rogers as a trick roper and vaudeville performer, before he went on to become one of the most famous Americans of his era. A tour guide may point out that the cowboy star, who was one-quarter Cherokee, was never a gun enthusiast. He refused to own guns or even carry them in movie roles. The animal pelts on view at his house were all gifts, as he never hunted.

The grounds of Will Rogers State Park include meadows and hiking trails, such as

Left: Will Rogers and family relax in the ranch house living room. Opposite: Goats graze on a hillside on the Rindge ranch. The Rindge family held all of Malibu as private property until construction of the coast highway began in 1925.

In nearby Rustic Canyon, a high-spirited group of leading citizens dubbed themselves "The Uplifters" and built a clubhouse on the site of a former forestry station, where they put on skits and plays and happily ignored Prohibition. Among them were Harold Lloyd, Busby Berkeley, and *Wizard of Oz* author L. Frank Baum. The clubhouse still stands as part of the Rustic Canyon Recreation Center, where arts and athletic classes are held for residents of the surrounding sylvan glade, a woodsy, creekside residential area full of million-dollar homes.

the popular short hike to Inspiration Point, which overlooks much of Santa Monica and the coast. A luxurious stable stands a short ride from the polo field. Polo matches still take place on weekend afternoons in summer and are open to the public, giving visitors the feeling they are walking into a piece of a pampered and privileged era of long ago.

On the opposite side of Sunset Boulevard, other lasting developments were taking place in the 1920s. The Riviera Country Club, with its golf course and polo fields, was established in 1927 and went on to host equestrian events during the 1932 Olympics.

....
Above: Members of "The Uplifters" polo club take the field in the 1920s. Right: Aerial view of polo field on Will Rogers estate. Top right: Golfers putt out at the Riviera Country Club.

Lake Shrine of the Self-Realization Fellowship

Just before Sunset Boulevard ends, it offers a rest stop of divine proportions, the Lake Shrine of the Self-Realization Fellowship, where travelers can linger to restore their equilibrium and take a break for contemplation. Dedicated and opened to the public in 1950, the Lake Shrine is the westernmost temple of the fellowship founded by Paramahansa Yogananda. (An earlier site was founded on Sunset Boulevard in East Hollywood, and another on Mount Washington.)

With its white walls and gold minaret towers, the temple rises like a mirage on the left as Sunset loops around the lake before reaching its end. (The place is difficult to miss, but entering the free parking lot requires

doubling back after a left turn.)

The grounds are a remarkable 10-acre sanctuary of beauty and tranquillity. A Court of All Religions illustrates the fellowship's universal approach to spiritual seeking. Visitors can walk the entire circumference of the lake and gardens, passing

. . . .

Above: Lotus plants reappear on Sunset Boulevard at the tranquil Lake Shrine of the Self-Realization Fellowship. Left: The order was founded by Paramahansa Yogananda, a native of India who spent more than 30 years in the U.S., shown in 1950 with California Lt. Governor and Mrs. Goodwin J. Knight at the dedication of the Lake Shrine and the Gandhi World Peace memorial.

The Intellectuals

In the 1930s, Pacific Palisades became known as a magnet for intellectual émigrés from Europe. Adolf Hitler's rise to power and the German invasion of Austria were spurring a generation of artists, writers, and composers to seek a safe harbor in America. Employment in Hollywood attracted some. Others, able to live on the royalties from works already produced, sought a more genteel way of life and found it in the Mediterranean clime and clubby seclusion of the Palisades.

European literary giants Leon Feuchtwanger and Thomas Mann became important figures in the social and intellectual life of the area, as did Aldous Huxley and his wife, Maria. Writer and theatrical director Berthold Viertel and his wife, Salka, were early arrivals from Europe; their house at 165 Mabery Road, near the mouth of Santa Monica Canyon, became a salon of sorts. Writer Christopher Isherwood occupied their garage apartment for a time, and Greta Garbo, for whom Salka wrote screenplay roles, was a frequent guest. Writer Robert Parrish observed that he arrived at the Viertel house one day to find Arthur Rubinstein playing the piano, Garbo lying on the sofa, Isherwood in a chair, and Bertolt Brecht cooking in the kitchen. Other frequent guests included composers Arthur Schoenberg, Oscar Levant, and Igor Stravinski, who lived in the area, and Billy Wilder, Charlie Chaplin, and Stella Adler.

Americans, including artist Edward Hopper and writer Henry Miller, also contributed to the Palisades' intellectual life. Miller lived for more than 20 years in the Huntington Palisades section after leaving his home in Big Sur, and went on to teach at UCLA. Industrial designers Charles and Ray Eames and inventor and engineer Buckminster Fuller are among other innovative and influential thinkers who lived in the Palisades.

originally designed as a Twentieth Century Fox movie prop, that Paramahansa Yogananda used as a meditation site. A small museum helps illustrate the yogi's life and beliefs. Last but not least, there are restrooms—a blessing in themselves.

Inceville

Years before Will Rogers came to stay, there was a tradition of cowboy play-acting at the western end of Sunset. Filmmaker Thomas Ince, considered "the father of the western," established his movie studio in 1911 at the mouth of Santa Ynez Canyon, where today Sunset Boulevard runs through to the ocean. By 1913, the studio he called "Inceville" had become a minor wonderland in the wilderness, a busy municipality with its own post office and as many as 700 employees. In all, Ince had 18,000 acres of spectacular scenery at his disposal. Sets were constructed for everything from a pirate ship to a Swiss village to a Puritan settlement. Even a few Keystone Kops "cliffhangers" were filmed in the vicinity, with the hapless comics hanging from cars tipping over the Palisades bluffs.

But it was in western movies that Ince made his mark. He hired an entire traveling

chapels and benches, a waterfall, and a sarcophagus containing ashes of the late world spiritual leader Mahatma Ghandi.

The sites also includes a reproduction of a 16th century Dutch windmill, where services were formerly held, and a houseboat,

Wild West Show, including a Sioux Indian tribe, to provide authenticity and action, and hired cowboy star William S. Hart to act in and direct many of the movies. Ince took a disciplined, efficient approach to movie making that was widely imitated as the studio system began to emerge. In 1915, he forged a coalition with two other leading filmmakers, D.W. Griffith and Mack Sennett, to form Triangle Pictures. The operations of all three "geniuses" were strung along Sunset Boulevard.

Inceville thrived until at least 1919, when Ince, like Griffith, invested in an anti-war masterpiece, *Civilization*, that came out just as sentiment was gathering for the first World War. The movie flopped, leaving Ince in financial straits. The oceanside studio had other problems, too; summertime fog at the beach interfered with filming and cut into profits. The buildings at Inceville were gradually abandoned. On the Fourth of July in 1922, a fire broke out and burned down everything except a church, which remained standing among the ruins on the beach for several

········

The Inceville movie studio in 1915, at the mouth of Santa Ynez Canyon, where today Sunset Boulevard meets the sea.

more years. Meanwhile, Ince had built a new studio in Culver City, adjacent to the lot that became MGM and is currently Sony Pictures Entertainment. The buildings are still in use today, on a street named for the filmmaker.

A few years later, in 1924, Ince died under mysterious circumstances aboard a yacht owned by newspaper magnate William Randolph Hearst, with whom he was in business negotiations. Ince, 43, had been celebrating his birthday at a party

onboard, along with fellow guest Charlie Chaplin and Hearst's paramour, Marion Davies. They had boarded the yacht at San Diego harbor. During the night, Ince was allegedly struck mortally ill and Hearst's private physician was summoned. At daylight, he was carried ashore on a stretcher, never to recover. A hasty cremation took place before authorities could examine the body, leading to speculation that a cover-up had been orchestrated by the powerful Hearst.

Drinking and gunplay—and an accidental shooting—were suspected by many in Hollywood. The most popular theory was that Hearst had shot at Chaplin, in a jealous rage over Davies, and had accidentally struck Ince. But according to Hearst's personal physician, who attended, Ince died of a heart attack. His widow was well provided for, and stuck to the official story even on her deathbed. But to this day, speculation persists.

At Home With the Reagans

Perhaps the most famous modern Palisades residents have been Ronald and Nancy Reagan, who built a house on San Onofre Drive in 1956. They held onto it even while Ron was California governor, visiting infrequently from Sacramento. In 1980, they were again occupying the house when he was elected president.

His triumph touched off a media circus and Secret Service invasion, with helicopters circling constantly overhead. San Onofre Drive was cordoned off, and motorcades of limousines and police cars carrying VIPs traveled constantly up and down Sunset Boulevard, causing no small inconvenience

Hiking the Palisades

With its access to the Santa Monica Mountains and ocean views, Pacific Palisades is a popular hiking destination. One of the most popular short hikes is at Will Rogers State Park, where trail signs point the way up the two-mile round-trip trail to a flat-topped knoll with views of Santa Monica Bay.

The Paseo Miramar trail is another popular and more ambitious hike (going west on Sunset, turn right on Paseo Miramar Drive, just past Palisades Drive and past the Lake Shrine, and follow it all the way to the top). The trail is five miles round trip, with a steep first mile that requires at least two hours' hiking time. Two miles up, at the first large fork, turn left toward the ocean for the most spectacular views of all from Parker Mesa Overlook. All of Santa Monica and the bay—including, at dusk, the so-called "Queen's necklace" of sparkling bayside lights—will be spread out before you. (Evening hikers will want to bring flashlights for the descent.) Views of Topanga State Park and the Santa Monica Mountains are among the rewards as the trail continues.

For a marvelous woodsy experience minus the altitude, try Santa Ynez Falls (drive up Palisades Drive to Verenda de la Montura, turn left and park near the signed trailhead). A gorgeous creekside ramble among coast live oaks, sycamores, and bay laurels, the trail nonetheless requires some boulder-hopping and stream-crossing to reach the falls, located less than 1.5 miles from the trailhead.

to residents. People magazine rounded up more than 2,000 Palisades residents for a community photograph, taken on Swarth-

....

Hikers can reach Eagle Rock in Topanga State Park from Palisades Drive off Sunset or through Will Rogers State Park.

more, just off Sunset Boulevard, under a banner reading "Home of Our 40th President."

Not until the Reagans sold their three-bedroom, all-electric home, which had been a gift built for them by General Electric while Ron was a company spokesman, did Pacific Palisades return to normal.

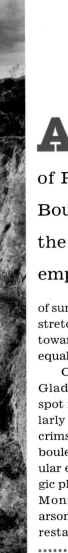

The Beach

At the end

of Pacific Palisades, Sunset
Boulevard at last descends to
the beach, like a fabled river
emptying into a delta mouth

of surf and sand. Crossing it at the terminus,
stretching north toward Big Sur and south
toward Mexico, is Pacific Coast Highway, an
equally romantic and far more scenic road.

On the sand where Sunset ends stands
Gladstone's 4 Fish, since 1972 a favored
spot for a beachside drink or meal, particularly during the magic hour panorama of
crimsons, golds, and purples for which the
boulevard was named. The fast-paced, popular eatery features a wall display of nostalgic photos of the beach culture of the Santa
Monica Bay, along with pictures of the
arson-set Malibu fires of 1993, for which the
restaurant served as an evacuation center

A dramatic view of the bluffs above Will Rogers State
Beach, shown in 1960, when the "Lighthouse" still
stood at the water's edge.

history had swung a different way.

More than a hundred years ago, the oceanfront just south of where Sunset now meets the sea contained an engineering marvel—a wharf nearly 5,000 feet long, the longest in the world. Railroad trains ran its length, carrying passengers and cargo to and from huge ships docked at its 130-foot-wide "harbor" end. From there, the incoming goods linked up to railroad tracks running along the coast and inland.

The "Long Wharf" was built in 1891 by the president of the Southern Pacific Railway, Collis P. Huntington, who hoped to secure a shipping monopoly in the region for his railroad. The need for a man-made, deep-water harbor to boost commerce in Los Angeles had become evident, and for 10 years Huntington waged a bitter campaign to make Santa Monica Bay the site where the necessary dredging would take place. Ultimately, and only after a protracted municipal battle that pitted some of the era's most powerful men against one another, city leaders chose to create a permanent harbor for the city 16 miles south at San Pedro.

••••••••••••••••••••••

A couple strolls the beach in front of Gladstone's restaurant. Opposite: Turn-of-the-century railroad officials pose on "the world's longest wharf" in Santa Monica Bay.

and firefighters' rest stop.

To the north are Malibu and Zuma beaches, the fabled playgrounds of celebrities and surfers. The state beach to the south, three miles long, was named in 1944 for Will Rogers, who once owned the land. South of that is the city of Santa Monica and its state beach and pier, with an amusement park and 1922 carousel, and beyond that, the carnival-like atmosphere of Ocean Front Walk in Venice. There are plenty of rental facilities for skates and bikes along

the Venice boardwalk, and few more joyous ways to relax than taking a spin along the coast's 22-mile paved recreational path, particularly near sunset, when the traffic usually fades away.

A favorite bench along the path always makes a sweet place to breathe in the ocean air and contemplate the gold and lavender hues of the sunset. And it's interesting to speculate how different the atmosphere in this curve of the Santa Monica Bay would be if a key industrial battle in Los Angeles

Work on the San Pedro harbor began in 1899, prompting a slow, steady decline of shipping at the Long Wharf. By 1913, its remains had been torn down, making way for the bay to become one of the region's most spectacular and popular beaches.

Set aside as a recreational area, Los Angeles County's coastline spawned a culture of its own. Trends such as sunbathing, surfing, beach volleyball, and body building were launched on these beaches, and helped create the mythical California image

A View from the Park, Santa Monica, Cal.

OVERLOOKING BEACH HOMES AND BEACH, SANTA MONICA, CALIFORNIA

MUNICIPAL PIER IN BACKGROUND

celebrated in songs, movies, and other avenues of pop culture.

The Hawaiian sport of surfing was introduced to California in 1907 by George Freeth, an Irishman born in Hawaii who had been hired by transportation magnate Henry Huntington (Collis' nephew) to help generate publicity for a seaside plunge located in Redondo Beach. Freeth put on the West Coast's first-ever surfing demonstrations, riding the waves for tourists twice a day on a short, heavy wooden surfboard. He later became the first official lifeguard in the Santa Monica Bay area. Freeth died while attempting an ocean rescue and is memorialized with a bust on the Redondo Beach Pier.

In the 1920s, the seashore was lined with private bath houses and "beach clubs," where paying patrons had access to showers, lockers, changing rooms, and snack bars. One such structure, the "Lighthouse," was located on the beach below the Palisades bluffs, across from the mouth of Potrero Canyon, at the same spot where the

Long Wharf formerly stood. Built in 1927, the Lighthouse contained a restaurant and changing rooms. It was used to lure prospective home buyers to the Palisades, as residents got free access to the club, and it became a landmark seen in many photographs from the era.

Employees and patrons of the clubs began developing much of what endures in Southern California beach culture. Beach volleyball was developed on courts at the various clubs and in the 1940s superseded surfing as the most popular sport at Santa Monica State Beach.

Two young Santa Monica lifeguards, Sam Reid and Tom Blake, helped spread the gospel of surfing in the 1920s after catching the bug in Hawaii. Reid and Blake worked the beach club circuit as lifeguards and devoted their spare time to surfing and developing innovations, such as a hollow paddleboard with a fin for added stability. Surfing gained more popularity in the 1950s, after Bob Simmons, a designer who had attended Caltech, introduced a lightweight board made of synthetic materials.

Surfers favored Malibu Beach in particular. It attracted a teenager named Kathy Kohner, drawn to both the boards and the boys. Her father, Frederick, a Hollywood scriptwriter, based his 1957 novel *Gidget* on her experiences at Malibu. The first *Gidget* movie, starring Sandra Dee as the "girl midget," came out in 1959 and scored a hit, luring more guys and girls to the scene. Also popular were the *Beach Party* films produced by American International Pictures, a teen exploitation outfit. The series of low-budgeters, some starring Annette Funicello and Frankie Avalon, was shot on the sands at Point Dume, north of Zuma. *Beach Blanket Bingo*, released in 1965, is generally considered the best of the lot, although *How to Stuff a Wild Bikini* had at least as good a title.

In the early 1960s, the brilliant pop tunes of the clean-cut Beach Boys, raised in the Los Angeles suburb of Downey, helped raise the profile of Southern California surfing, as hits like "Surfin' U.S.A." and "California Girls" got radio play all over the world.

"[A] wonderfully fresh...amusing, tough, and tender novel."
—*San Francisco Chronicle*

"Touching and entertaining."
—*The New York Times*

Gidget

Frederick Kohner

Foreword by Kathy Kohner Zuckerman,
✽ aka the real Gidget ✽
Introduction by Deanne Stillman

In more recent years, local beach and body culture has been mythologized in the hit TV series "Baywatch," the brainchild of a former L.A. County lifeguard, Greg Bonnan, who worked at Santa Monica Beach's Tower No. 18, where several episodes have been filmed. "Baywatch" nearly drowned early on, when NBC canceled it after one season. But Bonnan and three other producers swam in with star David Hasselhoff to produce it independently for syndication, and the lifeguard series took off. With its simple story lines and buff regulars—including world-class jiggler Pamela Anderson in red rescue togs—"Baywatch" became the most-watched television program in the world during its 12-year run, reportedly seen by more than a billion viewers in at least 110 countries.

The moody, atmospheric aspects of the coastal strip, just like their sunny counterparts, have been exploited by the purveyors of pop culture as well. Crime fiction writers like Raymond Chandler, James L. Cain, and Walter Mosley made use of the foggy piers as forlorn, gloomy places where private eyes were called to meetings with shadowy clients.

In Chandler's *The Big Sleep*, he describes Marlowe taking a hair-raising ride up the coast highway in a policeman's car, "using the siren once in a while to beat a signal," to arrive at the Malibu Pier, where a

dead man is being fished from the water. "We went out onto the pier, into a loud fish smell which one night's hard rain hadn't even dented," Chandler wrote. In the movie version of Mosley's *Devil in a Blue Dress*, Easy Rawlins (Denzel Washington) is called to a tense night-time rendezvous at the "Fisherman's Pier" in Malibu, where he endures racial harassment by white teenagers who are then frightened off by the appearance of his sociopath employer, Mr. Albright.

In real life, rum runners during Prohibition made daring use of the coast and the piers at Malibu and Santa Monica to smuggle ashore cases of illicit alcohol under cover of night and fog. The well-funded bootleggers plied their trade in high-powered speedboats that easily out-ran the decrepit vessels of the Coast Guard. Once the shipments came ashore, hijackings, double-crosses, and volleys of hot lead were not uncommon, meaning the crime fiction writers could draw plenty of inspiration from the day's newspapers. One of the boldest rum runners

was Tony Cornero, who parlayed his profits into gambling boats that operated for years outside the three-mile zone off Santa Monica Pier.

On a December night in 1935, a real-life film noir plot unfolded around the long, crumbling, Mediterranean-style building that still stands below the bluffs at 17575 Pacific Coast Highway, just before the stop light at Porto Marina. Then, it was called Thelma Todd's Sidewalk Cafe, named for the vivacious blonde comedienne popular in movies during the 1920s and 1930s, who ran it with her lover, movie producer Roland West.

The two shared an apartment above the cafe, and were heard arguing loudly that night after Todd returned from a Hollywood party. In the morning, her lifeless body, still dressed in jewels and furs, with its bloodied face, was found on the front seat of her Packard convertible. It was parked in her own garage, up the hill from the restaurant, with the engine running and the door closed. Though suicide seemed unlikely, the death was ruled accidental, from carbon monoxide poisoning.

There were rumors that Todd had been consorting with gangster Lucky Luciano and that she'd received threats on her life

after resisting gangland pressures to add a casino to her business. To the police, nothing added up. The mystery of her death was never solved. The cafe was shuttered, and the Castellammare area of Pacific Palisades, where it was located, took on an aura of foreboding and fear for years afterward.

The Japanese attack on Pearl Harbor on December 7, 1941, escalated tensions along the coast, as Southern California residents felt particularly vulnerable to an ocean invasion. The carefree attitude of the beach towns was replaced by grim paranoia. Air-raid sirens blared, and a blackout was strictly enforced after sundown. Along the beach, a citizen's militia was formed to guard

- - - - - - - - - - - - - - - - - - - -
Above: Thelma Todd's Cafe on the coast highway north of Sunset Boulevard, 1935. Right: Wartime bathers pose with an air-raid siren posted on a beach in the Santa Monica Bay, 1940s.

against enemy troops who might surface in submarines to invade by night. Barbed wire was strung up along Santa Monica State Beach, and 14 guard stations were established, staffed by men and women volunteers. U.S. Army battalions established armed camps in the area.

At 2:25 a.m. on February 25, 1942, citizens woke to the screaming of air-raid sirens, believing their worst fears had been realized. Searchlights scanned the sky along 10 miles of beachfront, then converged on a single spot. Anti-aircraft batteries hurled artillery skyward. Tracer bullets and exploding shells lit the sky, as hundreds of thousands of residents watched. Rumors flew that 15 enemy planes had been spotted and a secret enemy airbase uncovered on American

soil. But no planes were shot down that night, and no bombs were dropped. By dawn, an all-clear was sounded, and the secretary of the Navy reported a false alarm. No sound reason was ever given for the hysteria-inducing event.

Today, a former ammunition bunker is still visible in the base of the bluffs, just south of Will Rogers State Beach.

The Malibu Colony and The Coast Road

The Malibu colony of celebrity beachfront homes is part of L.A.'s lure and lore, along with the freedom to take a top-down spin along Malibu's 27 miles of coastline. But it wasn't always so.

From the turn of the century until the coast road opened in 1928, the land was privately owned by a family determined to deny access to the public. Millionaire Frederick Rindge and his wife, May Knight Rindge, bought the land for $10 an acre in 1892. They built a ranch, and for many years enjoyed splendid isolation. Travelers used the Rindges' ranch roads to pass through en route to points north. Even after a squatter's campfire set off a blaze that destroyed their ranch house, the Rindges allowed some access. But various abuses continued, and in 1917, a dozen years after her husband had died, May Knight Rindge closed the ranch roads and hired armed guards to defend against trespassers.

There followed a long and notorious battle that cost Mrs. Rindge more than $1 million in legal fees, as the state fought to establish

the right of eminent domain across "the Malibu." Even after the state won, the widow appealed, and her armed fence-riders turned back the engineers and surveyors who came to build a road. By 1925, when a superior

....

Teddy Roosevelt bust against coast highway bluffs, 1936. For a time, the highway carried his name.

court granted the state the right to start construction on Pacific Coast Highway, Mrs. Rindge was forced by financial pressures to give in. Nearly bankrupt, she began selling off beachfront lots to movie people, and the fabled "Malibu Colony" took shape. Bing Crosby, Gloria Swanson, Gary Cooper, and Barbara Stanwyck were among the first stars to build homes in the area.

The highway—then called the Roosevelt Highway, for Teddy Roosevelt—was completed and opened to traffic in 1928. Although sometimes closed by mudslides, fires, and other disasters, the coast road has become one of the most popular drives in Southern California, while the beaches at Malibu and Zuma are treasured by surfers, locals, and tourists. Ⓢ

Check it out: Pacific Palisades and the Beach

Food and Drink

Gladstone's 4 Fish, 17300 Pacific Coast Highway, (310) 573-0212. Lobster, fresh seafood, full bar, free peanuts, sunset views at a beachfront mainstay.

Kay 'n Dave's Cantina, 15246 Sunset Boulevard, (310) 459-8118. Local favorite. Bright, friendly spot for health-conscious Mexican food.

Modo Mio, 15200 Sunset Boulevard, (310) 459-0979. Italian trattoria favored by stars from surrounding hills.

Mort's Palisades Deli, 1035 Swarthmore Avenue, (310) 454-5511. Hang with the locals at a Palisades institution.

Patrick's Roadhouse, 106 Entrada Drive (at Pacific Coast Highway), (310) 459-4544. Casual daytime eatery. Weekend breakfasts popular with glitterati canyon-dwellers.

Reel Inn, 18661 Pacific Coast Highway, (310) 456-8221. Less expensive seafood dinners than at Gladstone's, and some say the fish is better. Short drive north on PCH from where Sunset meets the sea.

Rocco's, 17338 Sunset Boulevard,

(310) 573-3727. The best pizza around, per some locals.

TropiCal Bakery & Grill, 16905 Sunset Boulevard, (310) 459-9814. Coffee, pastries, breakfast, and lunch.

Books

Village Books, 1049 Swarthmore Avenue, (310) 454-4063. Cozy literary corner in heart of Pacific Palisades village. Features readings, good selection of local and Los Angeles writing.

Excursions

Will Rogers State Park and Polo Matches, 1501 Will Rogers State Park Road (just off Sunset in Pacific Palisades; signs point the way), (310) 454-8212. Park open daily; offers museum, house tours, hiking, picnicking. Polo matches played on historic field on weekends April through September, 2–5 p.m. Saturday and 10 a.m – 1 p.m. Sunday. Admission free to park and polo, no tickets required. Parking is $6. Information on rules of polo and how to watch a match: www.willrogerspolo.org.

Rustic Canyon Recreation Center, 601 Latimer Road, (310) 454-5734. Tennis, swimming, arts and crafts. Open to L.A. residents citywide.

Lake Shrine of the Self-Realization Fellowship, 17190 Sunset Boulevard, (310) 454-4114. Tranquil outdoor oasis for contemplation, prayer. Open 9 a.m.– 4:30 p.m. Tuesday-Saturday, 12:30–4:30 p.m. Sunday. Closed Mondays.

Postscript

At this point, the journey is complete. Sunset Boulevard has revealed itself—enough to fill a dozen weekends of exploration, a month of discovery-filled afternoons. The culmination of the trip deserves a bench facing the evening curtain show—that divine display of moody colors and gold-tipped clouds for which the Boulevard was named.

Such a respite can be found along the bike path that runs from Palos Verdes up to Will Rogers State Beach, or along the rails of the Santa Monica Pier, or beside the bluff-top paths of Palisades Park in Santa Monica.

From here, we can drink in the glorious and fleeting display of golds and reds, lavenders and blues that unfurls nightly in the western sky above the ocean, free for all to admire, even as most of us are too busy toiling at something else to even lift our heads.

At our backs will be not just Sunset Boulevard, but all of America—an entire nation full of towns and cities with scarcely a street as remarkable as the one we have just traversed.

Not many more than 100 years have passed since Sunset Boulevard first appeared on a map, and less than that since it was carved through the canyons near the beach. Yet it has borne witness to an incredible cavalcade of history and culture, and its unique energy, location, and aura of possibility have helped realize the aspirations of a parade of exceptional people. We can only try to imagine what another 100 years will bring, then point our own dreams into the sparkling nighttime city as we make an enlightened return trip down this remarkable boulevard. ◉

Acknowledgments

The author wishes to extend heartfelt appreciation and thanks to all the friends and colleagues who helped, including: Carla Lazzareschi, for conceiving the idea for this book and making it possible; Stacey Strickler and Mike Diehl, for making it look like I'd dreamed it would; Steven Hawkins, for judicious copy editing; the staff writers of the *Los Angeles Times*, for going before me on so many of these topics; the Los Angeles Public Library system, for its invaluable resources; and, for assistance along the way, Mike Bagheri, Murray Burns and Planaria Price, Federica Carrion, Diana Daniele, Janette Dean at *The Times* archives, John Duddy, Ron Emler, Greg Fischer, Vangie Griego and Greg Ptacek of the Silver Lake Film Festival, Tom LaBonge, Ernesto de la Loza, Suzanne Madrid, Karyn Millet, Eugene Moy, Danny Munoz, Robert Nudelman, Marcia Perloff, Leonard and Dale Pitt, Cecilia Rasmussen, John Rechy, Hynda Rudd, Tony Sears, Gloria Smith of the Brentwood Historical Society, Mark Wanamaker, Morgan Yates, and Randy Young.

Also, for abiding interest and enthusiasm, advice, or loans from their personal libraries, to Elizabeth M. Cosin, Jenny Cunningham, Judy Elkins, Jane Galbraith, David Kipen and Veronique de Turenne, Lynne Margulies, Amy McGary, Kristen McGary, Allison Robbins, Henry Schipper, James Valentine, and Tiare White. Special thanks to the Coffee Table in Silver Lake, where so many meetings were held.

Thanks most of all to my husband, Billy, whose support and kindness have been a constant blessing, whose adventurous exploration of this city is an inspiration, and whose humor and companionship are always a pleasure.

Photo Credits

All the images in this book are from the *Los Angeles Times* Editorial Library except for images on the following pages, which are courtesy of:

4   Nik Wheeler

7   Los Angeles Public Library, Photo Collection

8   Nik Wheeler

9   Los Angeles Times History Center

10   Adventure in Postcards

14   James Doolin

16   Regional History Center, Department of Special Collections, USC

17   El Pueblo of Los Angeles Historical Monument

18   Adventure in Postcards (Plaza Church); Bison Archives, Marc Wanamaker (Plaza in 1930s)

19   Nik Wheeler (all photographs)

21   El Pueblo of Los Angeles Historical Monument

22   Adventure in Postcards (Golden Pagoda)

23   Nik Wheeler

· · · · · · · · · · · · · · · · · ·

Opposite: Matchbook from the Good Luck Bar in Los Feliz (see page 79).

24   Los Angeles Public Library, Menu Collection

25   Nik Wheeler

26   Phillippe the Original

28   Stacey Rain Strickler

30   Automobile Club of Southern California

31   Suong Yangchareon

32   Bison Archives, Marc Wanamaker (both photographs)

34   Collection of Danny Munoz

35   Los Angeles Public Library, Photo Collection (children)

36   California State Library

37   Collection of Danny Munoz

38   ICFG Heritage Department

39   ICFG Heritage Department

40   Planaria Price

41   Nik Wheeler

44   Los Angeles Public Library, Photo Collection

45   California State University, Los Angeles, Holland Papers (letter); Regional History Center, Department of Special Collections, USC (eviction)

47   Los Angeles Public Library, Photo Collection

48   Air Photo Archives, UCLA Department of Geography

52   Judy Jones (Silver Lake); Bruce Torrence Historic Hollywood Collection (building the boulevard)

53   Bruce Torrence Historic Hollywood Collection

55   Stacey Rain Strickler (mural); Regional History Center, Department of Special Collections, USC (Sunset Bridge)

57   Bison Archives, Marc Wanamaker

58   Academy of Motion Picture Arts and Sciences

60   Bison Archives, Marc Wanamaker

62   Patricia Moritz and C.J. Bonura

64   Bison Archives, Marc Wanamaker

67   Los Angeles Public Library, Photo Collection

68   Academy of Motion Picture Arts and Sciences

69   Bison Archives, Marc Wanamaker

70   Academy of Motion Picture Arts and Sciences

72   Bison Archives, Marc Wanamaker

73   Los Angeles Public Library, Photo Collection (Fox Studios); Bison Archives, Marc Wanamaker (Scientific Films)

75   Academy of Motion Picture Arts and Sciences

76   Childrens Hospital of Los Angeles

77   Low Altitude Blimp Photography

78   Self-Realization Fellowship (temple)

82   Regional History Center, Department of Special Collections, USC

83   Nik Wheeler

84   Bruce Torrence Historic Hollywood Collection

85   Bison Archives, Marc Wanamaker (both photographs)

87   Adventure in Postcards

88   Adventure in Postcards (Brown Derby)

89   Los Angeles Public Library, Menu Collection (Moulin Rouge)

90   Nik Wheeler (both photographs)

92   Bison Archives, Marc Wanamaker (matchbook cover); California State Library (club building)

93   Bison Archives, Marc Wanamaker

94   Los Angeles Public Library, Photo Collection (Chaplin studios)

95   Bison Archives, Marc Wanamaker

97   Los Angeles Public Library, Photo Collection

98   Seaver Center for Western History Research

99   Nik Wheeler

100 Adventure in Postcards (Grauman's forecourt)

••••••••••••••••••••••••••••

Crossroads of the World and the Church of the Blessed Sacrament rise above Sunset Boulevard at Cherokee. Opposite, left: Union Station. Opposite, right: The Beverly Hills Hotel.

Bibliography

Aitken, Roy E. as told to Al P. Nelson. *The Birth of a Nation Story.* Middleburg, VA: A Denlinger Book, 1965.

Anger, Kenneth. *Hollywood Babylon.* New York: Simon & Schuster, 1975.

Bakalinsky, Adah and Larry Gordon. *Stairway Walks in Los Angeles.* Berkeley: Wilderness Press, 1990.

Balazs, Andre, ed. *Chateau Marmont Hollywood Handbook.* New York: Universe/Rizzoli Publications, 1996.

Basten, Fred E. *Beverly Hills: Portrait of a Fabled City.* Los Angeles: Douglas-West Publishing, 1975.

Blumenthal, John. *Hollywood High: The History of America's Most Famous Public School.* New York: Ballantine Books, 1988.

Bradley, Bill. *The Last of the Great Stations: 50 Years of the Los Angeles Union Passenger Terminal.* Glendale, CA: Interurban Publishing, 1989.

Brown, Karl. *Adventures With D.W. Griffith.* New York: Da Capo Press, 1973.

Byrnes, Edd with Marshall Terrill. *Edd Byrnes: "Kookie" No More.* New York: Barricade Books, Inc., 1996.

Caughey, John and LaRee Caughey. *Los Angeles: Biography of a City.* Berkeley: University of California Press, 1977.

Cheng, Suellen. *Chinatown Los Angeles: The Golden Years 1938-1988.* Los Angeles: Chinese Historical Society of Southern California, 1988.

Cini, Zelda and Bob Crane. *Hollywood: Land and Legend.* Los Angeles: Rosebud Books, Inc., for Arlington House Publishers, 1980.

Clark, David. *L.A. on Foot: A Free Afternoon.* Los Angeles: Camaro Publishing Co., 1972.

Clarke, Charles G. *Early Filmmaking in Los Angeles.* Los Angeles: Dawson's Book Shop, 1976.

Cobb, Sally Wright and Mark Willems. *The Brown Derby Restaurant: A Hollywood Legend.* New York: Rizzoli, 1996.

Dash, Norman. *Yesterday's Los Angeles.* Miami: Seemann Publishing, 1976.

Davis, Genevieve. *Beverly Hills: An Illustrated History.* Northridge, CA: Windsor Publications, 1988.

Davis, Margaret Leslie. *Childrens Hospital and the Leaders of Los Angeles: The First 100 Years.* Los Angeles: Childrens Hospital of Los Angeles Centennial Committee, 2002.

Dolby, Tom and Tina Hay, eds. *CityTripping: Los Angeles.* Los Angeles and New York: CityTripping Prods., Inc., 2000.

Emler, Ron. *Ghosts of Echo Park: A Pictorial History.* Los Angeles: Echo Park Publishing Co., 1999.

Epstein, Daniel Mark. *Sister Aimee: The Life of Aimee Semple McPherson.* San Diego and New York: Harcourt Brace & Co., 1993.

Fein, Art. *The L.A. Musical History Tour.* Los Angeles: 2.13.61 Press, 1998.

Warner brothers Harry, Jack, Sam, and Albert in 1929. Opposite: The Warner Bros. Studios—now home to television station KTLA—at Sunset and Van Ness.

Fleming, E.J. *Hollywood Death and Scandal Sites.* Jefferson, N.C., and London: McFarland & Co., 2000.

Grenier, Judson A., Doyce B. Nunis, and Jean Bruce Poole. *A Guide to Historic Places in Los Angeles County.* Dubuque, IA: Historical Society of Southern California, Kendall/Hunt Publishing, 1978.

Groper, Marilyn. *Highlights of Hollywood: A Self-Guided Tour.* Los Angeles: Self-Guided Tours Publishing, 1993.

Hancock, Ralph. *Fabulous Boulevard.* New York: Funk & Wagnalls Co., 1949.

Heimann, Jim. *Out With the Stars: Hollywood Nightlife in the Golden Era.* New York: Abbeville Press, 1985.

———. *Sins of the City: The Real L.A. Noir.* San Francisco: Chronicle Books, 1999.

Hentsell, Bruce. *Sunshine and Wealth: Los Angeles in the 1930s.* San Francisco: Chronicle Books, 1984.

Herman, Robert D. *Downtown Los Angeles: A Walking Guide.* Claremont, CA: City Vista Press, 1997.

Higham, Charles. *Warner Brothers.* New York: Charles Scribner's Sons, 1975.

Hirschorn, Clive. *The Columbia Story.* New York: Crown Publishers, 1990.

Horton, Joseph K. Based on a talk. *A Brief History of Bel-Air.* Los Angeles: Bel-Air Association, 1982.

Hoskyns, Barney. *Waiting for the Sun: Strange Days, Weird Scenes, and the Sound of Los Angeles.* New York: St. Martin's Griffin, 1999.

Hungry? A Guide to L.A.'s Greatest Diners, Dives, Cafeterias and Coffee Shops. Los Angeles: Really Great Books, 1999.

Johnson, Marael. *The National Geographic Traveler: Los Angeles.* Washington, D.C.: National Geographic Society, 2000.

Kaplan, Sam Hall. *L.A. Lost and Found: An Architectural History of Los Angeles.* New York: Crown Publishers, 1987.

Kennelley, Joe and Roy Hankey. *Sunset Boulevard: America's Dream Street.* Burbank, CA: Darwin Publications, 1981.

Lawson, Kristan and Anneli S. Rufus. *California Babylon: A Guide to Sites of Scandal, Mayhem, and Celluloid in the Golden State.* New York: St. Martin's Griffin, 2000.

Manchel, Frank. *When Pictures Began to Move.* New York: Prentice Hall, 1969.

Marinacci, Barbara and Rudy Marinacci. *Take Sunset Boulevard: A California Guide.* San Rafael, CA: Presidio Press, 1980.

Normark, Don. *Chavez Ravine, 1949: A Los Angeles Story*. San Francisco: Chronicle Books, 1999.

Pitt, Leonard and Dale Pitt. *Los Angeles A–Z: An Encyclopedia of the City and County*. Berkeley: University of California Press, 1997.

Rasmussen, Cecilia. *Los Angeles Unconventional: The Men and Women Who Did Los Angeles Their Way*. Los Angeles: Los Angeles Times, 1998.

Reavill, Gil. *Los Angeles*. Oakland, CA: Compass American Guides, 1992.

Regan, Michael. *The Mansions of Beverly Hills*. Los Angeles: Regan Publishing Co., 1966.

Robinson, David. *Hollywood in the Twenties*. London: A. Zwemmer Ltd., 1968.

Robinson, William and Lawrence Clark Powell. *The Malibu*. Los Angeles: The Ward Ritchie Press, 1958.

Sarlot, Raymond R. and Fred E. Basten. *Life at the Marmont*. Santa Monica, CA: Roundtable Publishing, 1987.

Schessler, Ken. *This Is Hollywood: An Unusual Movieland Guide*. U.S.A.: Ken Schessler, 1998.

Schickel, Richard. *D.W. Griffith: An American Life*. New York: Simon & Schuster, 1984.

Stanton, Jeffrey. *Santa Monica Pier: A History From 1875 to 1990*. Los Angeles: Donahue Publishing, 1990.

Stuart, Sandra Lee and John Prince. *The Pink Palace Revisited: Behind Closed Doors at the Beverly Hills Hotel*. Fort Lee, N.J.: Barricade Books, Inc., 1993.

Thomas, Bob. *Walt Disney: An American Original*. New York: Simon and Schuster, 1976.

Torrence, Bruce T. *Hollywood: The First Hundred Years*. New York: Zoetrope, 1982.

Wagner, Walter. *Beverly Hills: Inside the Golden Ghetto*. New York: Grosset & Dunlap, 1976.

Ward, Elizabeth and Alain Silver. *Raymond Chandler's Los Angeles*. Woodstock, N.Y.: The Overlook Press, 1987.

Wiener, Nina, ed. *Thirsty? A Guide to L.A.'s Cocktail Bars, Coffeehouses and Juice Bars*. Los Angeles: Glove Box Guides, 2000.

Wilder, Billy with an introduction by Jeffrey Meyers, *Sunset Boulevard: The Screenplay*. Berkeley: University of California Press, 1999.

Yates, Stephanie Avnet. *Frommer's 2000 Los Angeles*. New York: Macmillan USA, 2000.

Young, Betty Lou and Thomas R. Young. *Santa Monica Canyon: A Walk Through History*. Santa Monica, CA: Casa Vieja Press, 1997.

———. *Pacific Palisades: Where the Mountains Meet the Sea*. Los Angeles: Pacific Palisades Historical Society Press, 1983.

Young, Randy and Betty Lou Young. *Street Names of Pacific Palisades and Other Tales*. Los Angeles: Pacific Palisades Historical Society Press, 1990.

The southeast corner of Sunset and Crescent Heights, 1937, the original location of Schwab's Drugstore.

Index

Home restaurant on Hillhurst Avenue in Los Feliz.

• •

A red wooden bridge crosses the northeast tip
of Echo Park Lake.

There's frequently a line to get into the Sunset Room, a bar and supper club on Cahuenga just south of Sunset. Opposite: Comedy fans queue up at the Laugh Factory on Sunset near Crescent Heights.

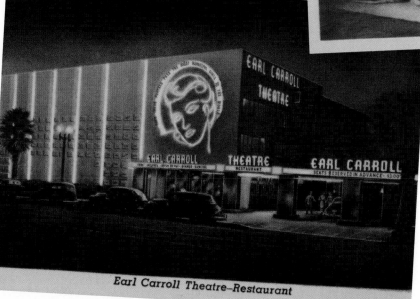

Earl Carroll Theatre–Restaurant

OTHER BOOKS FROM THE LOS ANGELES TIMES

DRAWING THE LINE
by Paul Conrad
Two hundred drawings, spanning the period from the late 1960s to President Clinton's impeachment trial, from America's premier political cartoonist. $25.45

ETERNALLY YOURS
by Jack Smith
Who can forget Jack Smith, the *Los Angeles Times'* columnist for nearly 40 years? When he died in 1996, we all lost a treasure. But at least his words survived. Here, Jack's widow, Denise, and his sons, Curt and Doug, have collected some of their favorite columns. $16.95

CURBSIDE L.A.
An Offbeat Guide to the City of Angels
by Cecilia Rasmussen
Enjoy a truly eclectic tour of Los Angeles. Explore the L.A. you've not seen with enticing excursions into the city's peerless history and diversity. $19.45

DAY HIKERS' GUIDE TO SOUTHERN CALIFORNIA
by John McKinney
Walks in Southern California, from the simply scenic to the challenging, as described by *Los Angeles Times* hiking columnist and author John McKinney. $16.45

....

Opposite: Perched on a hillside, the Hollywood sign overlooks the Hollywood Reservoir and, farther on, Sunset Boulevard.

52 WEEKS IN THE CALIFORNIA GARDEN
by Robert Smaus
How to make the most of your garden by the foremost authority on gardening in Southern California. $17.45

ANSWERS TO YOUR CALIFORNIA GARDENING QUESTIONS
by Robert Smaus
For decades, gardeners in Southern California turned to Robert Smaus, the *Los Angeles Times'* gardening editor, for practical, expert advice. This book is full of those questions and Smaus' authoritative answers. An excellent companion to *52 Weeks in the California Garden.* $21.45

HIGH EXPOSURE/ HOLLYWOOD LIVES
Found photos from the archives of the *Los Angeles Times*
by Amanda Parsons
In this beautiful hardcover book you'll see photographs of Marilyn Monroe, Liz Taylor, Mae West, Jane Russell, Frank Sinatra, Rita Hayworth, Errol Flynn and scores more stars at the height, and sometimes the depth, of their Hollywood lives. $29.95

IMAGING LOS ANGELES
Photographs of a 20th Century City
Foreword by Ray Bradbury
Collected here are some 175 photos from more than a dozen Southern California archives that tell the tale of men and women from all over the world who hoped and dared on a grand scale and who turned Los Angeles into the quintessential 20th century city. $28.95

L.A. UNCONVENTIONAL
by Cecilia Rasmussen
Where some people see roadblocks, others, such as the men and women in this volume, see possibility, opportunity and excitement. $30.95

THE SAN FERNANDO VALLEY
America's Suburb
by Kevin Roderick
Valley native Kevin Roderick recounts the area's vibrant past, from its Native American residents through the Spanish, Mexican and American settlers, spinning along the way the tales that give the Valley its unique history and culture. $26.45

LAST OF THE BEST
90 Columns from the 1990s
by Jim Murray
The best of Jim's columns from the last decade of his life are included in this paperback volume compiled by *Los Angeles Times* Sports Editor Bill Dwyre and featuring a foreword by Dodger legend Tommy Lasorda. $19.45

THE GREAT ONES
by Jim Murray
The top men and women of the sports world written about as only this late, great sports columnist could. Foreword by Arnold Palmer. $24.45

LOW-FAT KITCHEN
by Donna Deane
From the pages of the *Los Angeles Times* Food section come more than 110 recipes that use fresh food flavor, not fat, to satisfy your taste buds. $20.45

THE LOS ANGELES TIMES' MODERN CALIFORNIA COOKING
Staff of The Times' Food section
A sequel to the 1981 best seller, *California Cookbook, Modern California Cooking* offers more than 300 recipes that reflect the cutting edge, international cuisine for which Southern California has become so famous in recent years. An ideal companion to the 1981 volume. $22.45

SOS RECIPES
30 Years of Requests
by Rose Dosti
This best-selling hard-cover book offers hundreds of tried-and-true recipes for all-time favorite dishes that literally range from soup to nuts. $19.45

DEAR SOS/FAVORITE RESTAURANT RECIPES
by Rose Dosti
Rose Dosti has culled her perennially popular column in the *Los Angeles Times* Food section to hand pick 225 of your all-time favorite recipes from restaurants throughout the country. $22.45

To order, call (800) 246-4042 or visit our web site at http://www.latimes.com/bookstore